Dwayne's Guitar Lessons Presents:

Beginner's Guide to Lead Guitar Mastery

Unlock Secrets of the Fretboard

By
Guitar Teacher
Dwayne Jenkins

Introduction

Welcome to your journey toward mastering the art of lead guitar. This guide is structured to help you systematically develop your skills, with a focus on both technique and creativity.

As you embark on your journey, it's important to recognize that learning this instrument is a multifaceted process. It's not just about hitting the right notes; it's about expressing emotion, telling a story, and connecting with your audience.

The path to becoming a proficient lead guitarist is filled with both challenges and triumphs, demanding dedication and a willingness to explore new musical territories. This guide aims to provide you with the tools and knowledge needed to pursue your musical aspirations with confidence and creativity.

One of the key elements of this journey is developing a strong technical foundation. Techniques such as alternate picking, hammer-ons, pull-offs, and string skipping are essential for playing complex solos with precision and flair.

Equally important to technical skills is the creative aspect of improvisation. An art form that allows you to express your individuality and emotions. This guide will explore various techniques needed to do so.

These tools will enable you to craft compelling solos and melodies that resonate with your audience, turning your guitar into an extension of your voice. Embrace the chance to experiment, take risks, and find your unique sound.

You'll discover that effective practice habits and a positive mindset are essential components of successful learning. Setting clear goals, maintaining regular practice routines, and embracing challenges will ensure continuous growth.

Remember, the journey to mastery is ongoing, and each step you take brings you closer to realizing your full potential as a lead guitarist. Celebrate your progress, share your passion with others, and let the joy of music guide you on this exciting and transformative path. Have patience, practice daily, and have fun.

Sincerely, Dwayne Jenkins

Table of Contents

Chapter I: Foundation of Lead Guitar

Lesson 1: Role of the Lead Guitarist

The lead guitarist is often seen as the band's star, responsible for delivering captivating solos and memorable melodies. However, the role goes far beyond the spotlight.

A lead guitarist must have a deep understanding of musical dynamics, contributing to the overall sound and feel of the band's performance.

Rhythm and Melody

- **Rhythmic Interaction:** While primarily focused on melody, the lead guitarist must be adept at interacting rhythmically with other band members. This includes complementing the rhythm guitarist and maintaining cohesion with the drummer and bassist.

- **Melodic Contribution:** The lead guitarist delivers expressive, emotive solos that enhance the song's story. Understanding scales and modes is crucial to crafting melodies that resonate with the audience.

The neck is typically made of wood and may include a truss rod to adjust its curvature.

Essential Skills for a Lead Guitarist

To excel as a lead guitarist, one must develop a set of core skills that are both technical and creative. These skills lay the foundation for delivering dynamic performances and meaningful contributions to the band's sound.

- **Technical Proficiency:** Mastery of techniques such as alternate picking, bends, slides, and vibrato is essential.

These techniques allow the lead guitarist to express and execute their musical prowess with precision.

- **Creativity and Improvisation:** A great lead guitarist is also an innovative musician who can improvise on the spot.

This involves having a vast repertoire of licks and the ability to seamlessly weave them into solos.

- **Listening and Adaptability:** Being a successful lead guitarist requires a keen ear for music and the ability to adapt to various musical styles and situations.

This includes listening to other musicians and understanding how to blend or stand out as needed.

By understanding these basic fundamentals, you will develop a solid foundation in lead guitar playing. Allowing future lessons you study to stand on.

4

Lesson 2: The Musical Alphabet

Understanding the musical alphabet is fundamental for any guitarist aiming to excel in lead guitar. This lesson will cover the basics of musical notes and their application to the guitar fretboard, providing a solid foundation for further studies.

The Basics of the Musical Alphabet

The musical alphabet consists of seven primary notes: A, B, C, D, E, F, and G. These notes repeat in a cycle and are the foundation for all music theory. Each note can also have a sharp (#) or flat (b) variant, leading to a total of twelve distinct pitches in Western music.

- **Natural Notes**: The notes without sharps or flats (A, B, C, D, E, F, G) are known as natural notes.

Understanding their sequence and how they appear on the guitar fretboard is crucial for identifying scales and chords.

A through G are the basic seven notes of the musical alphabet; once you add the sharps or flats, it brings it to twelve magical notes.

- **Sharps and Flats:** Sharps raise a note by a half step, while flats lower a note by a half step. For example, A# is a half step above A, and Bb is a half step below B.

A sharp and a flat are the same; it just depends on which way you are moving along the fretboard. So C sharp is going to be the same as D flat. Recognizing these variations is essential for playing in different keys and modes.

The 12 magical notes of the musical alphabet are:

A–A#/Bb–B–C–C#/Db–D–D#/Eb–E–F–F#/Gb–G–G#/Ab

1　 2　 3 4　 5　 6　 7　 8 9　 10　 11　 12

If you look closely, you'll see that the notes are sharp if you go o from A to G, and they're flat if you go the other way. You also want to make sure to notice and remember that the B and E do not have a sharp or flat after them.

Applying the Musical Alphabet

Once you grasp the basic concept of the musical alphabet, the next step is to apply it to your instrument. This knowledge is essential for locating notes on the fretboard and understanding how scales and chords are constructed.

- **Fretboard Layout:** The guitar fretboard is a grid that maps the musical alphabet in half-steps. Familiarize yourself with the note positions across all six strings, starting with the open strings: E, A, D, G, B, and E.

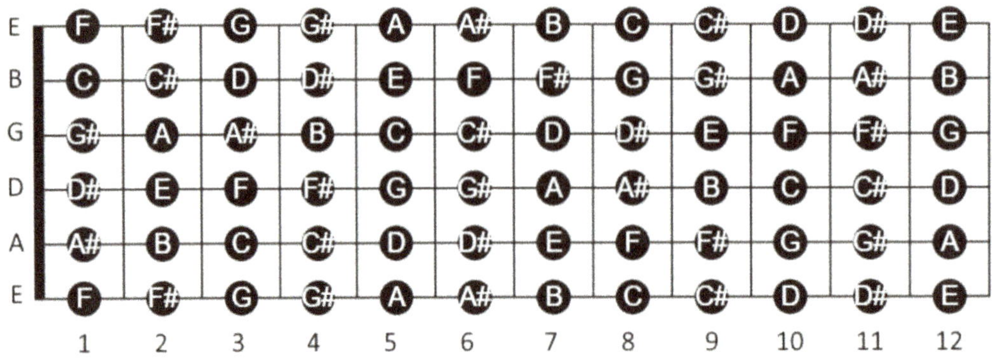

Notice how the musical alphabet is on each string, and each string follows the same pattern. The only difference is where it starts depends on which string you start it from. Go through each string and memorize the location of each note.

Lesson 3: Alternate Picking

Alternate picking is a fundamental technique for any aspiring lead guitarist. This lesson will break down the technique into two essential topics to help you develop speed, accuracy, and fluency in your playing.

The Mechanics of Alternate Picking

This technique uses a consistent up-and-down motion with the pick, allowing for more efficient, fluid playing than down-strokes alone. Mastering this technique is vital for playing fast passages and complex solos.

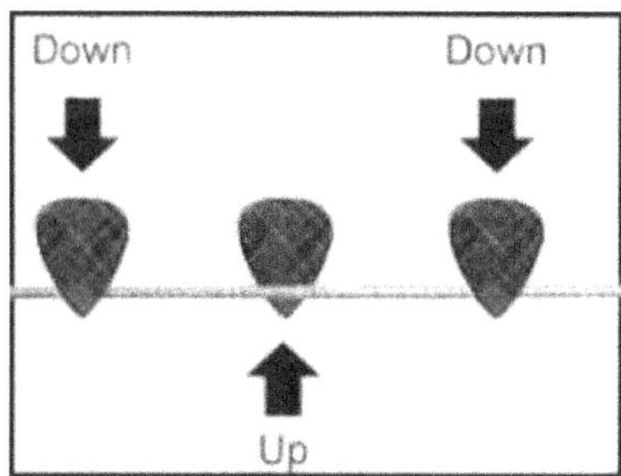

As you can see from the picture, you first pick down, then up, and back down again. As opposed to just picking down on all strikes. Not only can this allow for quicker playing, but it can also be used for intricate rhythms.

- **Basic Technique:** Start by holding the pick between your thumb and index finger, with a comfortable grip that allows for movement. The picking motion should come primarily from the wrist, not the arm, to maintain control and minimize fatigue.

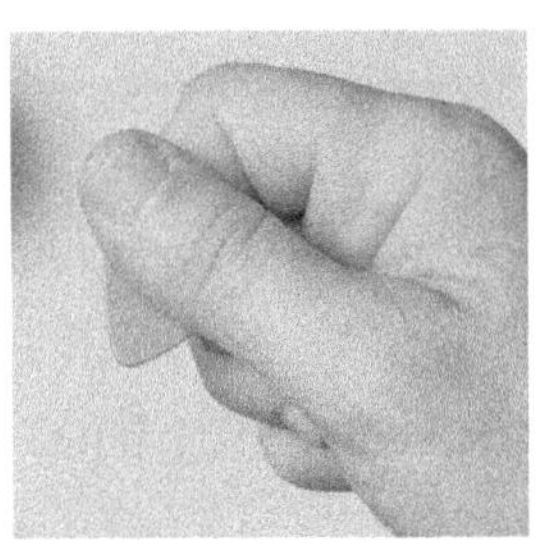 

- **Economy of Motion:** Focus on keeping the pick's motion small and precise. The less distance the pick travels, the faster and more accurately you can play.

Begin with simple exercises on open strings to establish a steady rhythm, then gradually increase the speed.

Practicing Alternate Picking

Practicing scales is an excellent way to apply alternate picking and improve your technical skills. It not only reinforces the picking motion but also helps you become familiar with the fretboard and scale patterns.

- **Scale Patterns**: Start with a simple scale, such as the C major scale. Practice playing it ascending and descending with alternate picking, ensuring each note is clear and evenly timed.

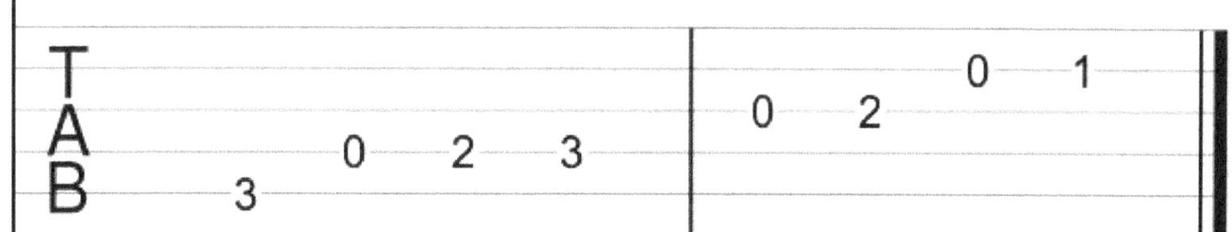

This scale will be presented later in the training when you learn to read guitar notation. By learning to read notation, you'll be able to learn scales quickly as well as gradually incorporate more complex scales as you become comfortable.

- **Metronome Practice:** Use a metronome to develop timing and consistency. Begin at a slow tempo, focusing on clean notes and precise picking.

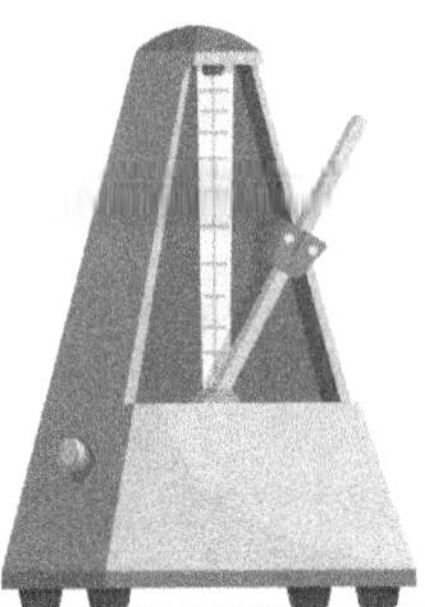

There are many different types of metronomes, and you can even find one on your computer. The one above is the most popular, but there are also more compact ones.

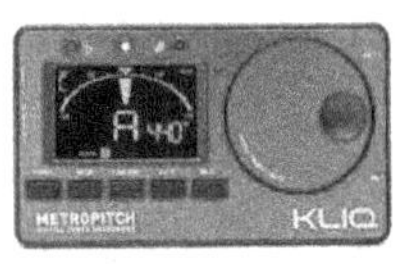

As you improve, slowly increase the tempo to challenge your speed and accuracy. This methodical approach helps embed alternate picking into your muscle memory, which is essential for advanced playing.

Chapter I Quiz

In Chapter 1, we covered the basics of lead guitar. Your role as a lead guitarist, the musical alphabet, and alternate picking. All of which set a solid foundation.

Q: What is the main responsibility of the lead guitarist?
A: ____

Q: What crucial skills are needed as a proficient lead guitarist?
A: ____

Q: What are the twelve primary notes in the musical alphabet?
A: ____

Q: What is the difference between a flat and a sharp note?
A: ____

Q: What is the primary motion used in alternate picking?
A: ____

Q: How can practicing with a metronome be beneficial?
A: ____

Chapter I Summary

<u>First</u>, you learn about your role as a lead guitarist. The lead guitarist is often seen as the band's star, responsible for delivering captivating solos and memorable melodies. However, the role goes far beyond that.

<u>Second,</u> you learn about the twelve magical notes called the musical alphabet. Fundamental for any guitarist looking to excel at playing lead guitar. These twelve notes can be used to create scales and chords.

<u>Third</u>, you learn how to apply the musical alphabet across the fretboard. Remember, the musical alphabet resides on each of the six strings and should be committed to memory.

<u>Fourth</u>, you learn about alternate picking. Where you pick the string in an up-and-down motion. This is a very common technique for playing guitar solos. That is why it is presented so early in the training.

<u>Lastly</u>, these first few lessons will provide a solid foundation for your lead guitar playing. Knowing your role, knowing the musical alphabet, and mastering alternate picking.

Chapter II: Basic Lead Guitar Scales

Lesson 4: The Major Scale

The major scale is one of the most fundamental building blocks in music theory and is essential for any lead guitarist. This lesson will explore the intricacies of the major scale, providing a solid foundation for understanding musical harmony and constructing melodies.

Structure and Theory of the Major Scale

Understanding the structure and theoretical aspects of the major scale is crucial for any musician. This topic will delve into the components that make up the scale and its broader musical significance.

- **Scale Formula**: The major scale follows a specific pattern of whole and half steps: Whole, Whole, Half, Whole, Whole, Whole, Half.

This pattern creates the familiar sound of the major scale, which is both uplifting and harmonious.

- **Degrees of the Scale:** Each note in the major scale is given a degree, numbered from one to seven. The first degree is the tonic, which serves as the home base of the scale. Understanding these degrees is vital for building chords and creating melodies.

Major Scale Degrees:

1. Tonic: The root note, foundation of the scale
2. Supertonic: One whole step above the tonic
3. Mediant: Middle note between the tonic and dominant
4. Subdominant: A perfect fourth above the tonic
5. Dominant: The fifth note, crucial for stability
6. Submediant: Middle note between subdominant and tonic
7. Leading Tone: A half step below the octave/tonic

C Major Scale = C D E F G A B octave

1 2   3 4 5   6   7

As you can see from what is presented above, the C note of the C major scale will be the Tonic, the G note will be the Dominant, and so forth. This applies to all major scale tone degrees.

Playing the Major Scale on Guitar

Mastering the major scale on the guitar is a practical step that will enhance your ability to improvise and compose. This topic will focus on the application of the major scale on the fretboard.

- **Fretboard Pattern:** Learn the common finger patterns used to play the major scale on the guitar. Start with the C major scale in open position, then explore movable patterns that can be used in any key.

Familiarity with these patterns will enable you to play the major scale across the entire fretboard.

- **Connecting Scale Patterns:** Practice connecting different scale patterns smoothly. This will help in creating seamless transitions during solos and improvisations.

By understanding the theoretical foundation and applying the major scale to your playing, you will gain the proficiency needed to tackle more advanced musical concepts, such as chord progressions and modal improvisation, which are integral parts of a lead guitarist's toolkit.

Lesson 5: The Natural Minor Scale

The natural minor scale is a fundamental scale for lead guitarists, offering a contrasting mood to the major scale. Understanding and mastering this scale will greatly enhance your ability to convey a range of emotions through your music.

Structure and Theory of the Natural Minor Scale

- **Scale Formula**: The natural minor scale follows a specific sequence of whole and half steps: Whole, Half, Whole, Whole, Half, Whole, Whole.

This pattern gives the scale its characteristic melancholic, sad, and introspective sound.

- **Degrees of the Scale**: Each note in the natural minor scale is assigned a degree from one to seven. The first degree is the tonic, which anchors the scale.

Just like the major scale, understanding these degrees is crucial for constructing chords and developing musical phrases in minor keys.

Minor Scale Tone Degrees:

1. First Degree: The root of the scale
2. Second Degree: A whole step up from the root
3. Flat Third Degree: A half step up from the second
4. Fourth Degree: A whole step up from the third
5. Fifth Tone Degree: A whole step up from the fourth
6. Flat Sixth Degree: A half step up from the fifth
7. Flat Seventh Degree: A whole step up from the sixth

A minor Scale: A   B   C   D   E   F   G

1   2   b3   4   5   b6   b7

By flattening the 3rd, 6th, and 7th tone degrees, you create an altered scale from the major, the natural minor. Just like the major, these flattened notes apply to all natural minor scales.

I say natural, because when some of the natural minor scale notes are altered, other types of minor scales are created. Which will be gone over later in the training.

For now, just focus on mastering the major and natural minor scale note formulas.

Playing the Natural Minor Scale on Guitar

Applying the natural minor scale to the guitar is crucial for improvisation and composition. This topic will guide you through playing the scale across the fretboard.

- **Fretboard Pattern**: Start by learning the A natural minor scale fretboard pattern, which shows how it looks across the fretboard.

Once comfortable, explore moving the scale pattern around. This allows you to play the natural minor scale in any key. Familiarity with the pattern will make it easier for you to navigate the fretboard.

- **Connecting Scales**: Once you've learned other minor scale patterns (which will be learned later in the training), work at connecting them to master transposing keys and fretboard mastery.

As you practice, focus on maintaining a consistent tone and rhythm across the entire range of the scale.

Lesson 6: Relative Major Minor Theory

Understanding the relationship between major and minor scales is crucial for any lead guitarist. This lesson will explore how these scales are interconnected, enhancing your ability to create more nuanced and emotive music.

The Circle of Fifths and Scale Relationships

To fully grasp the concept of relative major and minor scales, it's essential to understand the Circle of Fifths and how scales relate to one another. This knowledge provides a smooth transition between major and minor keys.

The circle of fifths is a visual clock-like diagram in music theory that arranges the 12 keys by their relationships to one another. Ascending and descending intervals help musicians understand key signatures and determine which major keys are relative to which minor keys.

By moving clockwise, you find each key a perfect fifth apart. Understanding this helps with relative major minor theory.

- **Circle of Fifths:** This visual tool illustrates the relationships among the 12 major keys and their relative minor keys.

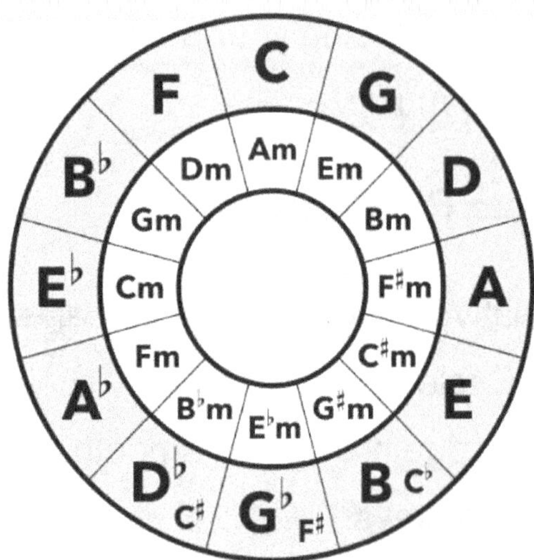

The key you start with is C major, and moving clockwise, the letters are represented a fifth apart. G is a fifth apart from C, D is a fifth apart from G, A is a fifth apart from D, and E is a fifth apart from A.

The inner circle tells you which key is the relative minor to the major key that is in the bigger circle. Can you see how helpful this diagram can be as a reference guide?

- **Relative Scales:** Every major scale has a relative minor scale that shares the same key signature. For example, C major and A minor are relative scales. The relative minor is located three half steps below its major counterpart.

8   5

The C note (which is the root of C major) is located at the 8th fret. If you move down the fretboard by three frets, you will end up on the 5th fret. This is where the A note is located, which is the root note of A minor. These two keys are related because they are built on the same notes.

C Major: C D E F G A B = 1 2 3 4 5 6 7

A minor: A B C D E F G = 1 2 b3 4 5 b6 b7

When you look at the two scales, you can clearly see that the notes are the same. This is why they are relevant.

Let's look at this with a couple more keys, then go back to the circle of fifths diagram and see if it's correct.

G Major: G A B C D E F# = 1 2 3 4 5 6 7

E Major: E F# G# A B C# D# = 1 2 3 4 5 6 7

E Minor: E F# G A B C D = 1 2 b3 4 5 b6 b7

Can you see how, when you change the E major key to E minor, the notes become the same as G major? This tells us that G major and E minor are relative to each other.

D Major: D E F# G A B C# = 1 2 3 4 5 6 7

B Major: B C# D# E F# G# A# = 1 2 3 4 5 6 7

B minor: B C# D E F# G A = 1 2 b3 4 5 b6 b7

Once again, you can clearly see that when we make the B major into the B minor, the notes become the same as the D major. This tells us that the D major and the B minor are related.

Why is this important to know?

Because it lets us switch seamlessly between these two keys (and chords), and they will sound good every time because they're made up of the same notes.

Applying Relative Major and Minor Theory on Guitar

Applying this theory to the guitar enables you to switch effortlessly between major and minor sounds, enriching your musical expression and improvisational skills.

- **Identifying Relative Scales on the Fretboard**: Begin by locating a major scale pattern on the fretboard, such as the C major scale. The relative minor, A minor, starts on the 6th degree of the major scale.

C Major: C D E F G A B = 1 2 3 4 5 6 7

The A note is in the 6th position of the key of C major. This tells us that the 6th note of this major scale is the relative minor.

G Major: G A B C D E F# = 1 2 3 4 5 6 7

Once again, the E note is located in the 6th position of the key of G major. This lets us know that E is the relative minor key.

Practice finding these relative positions for various keys to become adept at switching between them.

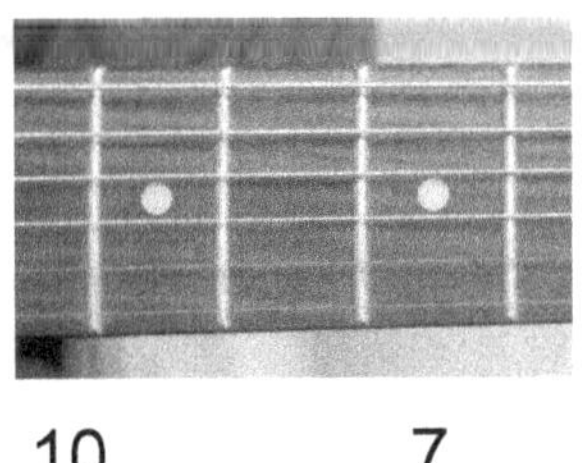

In this example, the D note is located at the 10th fret, and the B note is located at the 7th fret. If you were playing D major, you could switch down three frets to B minor and still sound good.

The Opposite Direction

This also works in the opposite direction. If you are playing a minor key, such as G minor, you could move up three frets to the relative major.

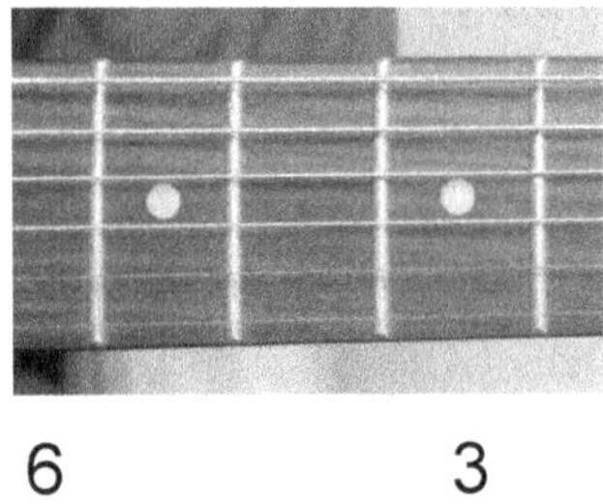

If you play G minor at the third fret, the relative major will be up three frets, just like going from major to minor, except in the opposite direction. Knowing this secret will make it easy to quickly find these two scales in any key on the fretboard.

If the relative minor is located at the 6th position in the major key, is the relative major key located within a minor?

Yes, it is. But where?

Well, let's take a look.

A minor: A B C D E F G = 1 2 b3 4 5 b6 b7

Now, since we know that A minor is the relative minor key to C major, all we need to do is find that note within the scale. As we can clearly see, it is in the 3rd position.

So, this tells us that the relative major key in any minor key is in the third position.

Is this correct with all minors?

Let's find out.

B minor: B C# D E F# G A = 1 2 b3 4 5 b6 b7

Once again, we know that B minor is the relative minor key to D major, and just like before, the relative major key is in the 3rd position of the minor.

So we can conclude that the relative major is the 3rd note.

- **Practical Application**: Use popular chord progressions to practice transitioning between relative major and minor scales. For example, try moving from a G major chord to an E minor chord and carefully listen to how they sound together.

G major   E minor

This exercise will enhance your ability to hear how these two relative keys work together harmoniously in music.

Remember, the two chords sound good together because they share the same notes.

The G major triad is G B E, and the E minor triad is E G B.

Notice how they are the same. If they sound together in chord format, they will also sound together in scale format.

Chapter II Quiz

In Chapter 2, you have learned about the major scale, the minor scale, and relative major minor theory. All of which are critical to the foundation of your lead guitar development.

Q: What is the major scale whole step half step formula?

A: ____

Q: What is the function of the tonic note in the major scale?

A: ____

Q: What is the minor scale whole step, half step formula?

A: ____

Q: What best describes the sound of the natural minor scale?

A: ____

Q: What is the relative minor scale of the C major scale?

A: ____

Q: What is the benefit of learning about the circle of fifths?

A: ____

Chapter II Summary

First, you learn the major scale. The major scale is one of the most fundamental building blocks in music theory and is essential for any lead guitarist. This scale will serve as the basis for all subsequent scales.

Second, you learn about the structure and theory of the major scale. The whole step, half step formula, and the degrees of the scale. The tonic, supertonic, and so forth. Knowing these concepts will develop your musicality.

Third, you learn about the natural minor scale. The counterpart to the major. This is where you alter the notes of the major scale to create a different shade of color. The natural minor scale will be the basis for all other minor scales.

Fourth, you learn about relative major minor theory. This concept involves two scales made up of the same notes. One major and one minor that work well together. This concept can deeply enhance your ability to create memorable music.

Lastly, by developing a strong sense of these scale concepts, you will lay a solid foundation for your musicality and for creating solos and melodies.

Chapter III: Reading Guitar Notation

Lesson 7: Reading Charts and Diagrams

Reading charts and diagrams is an essential skill for any guitarist, as it allows you to quickly comprehend and interpret musical information.

This lesson will focus on understanding chord charts and scale diagrams, providing you with the tools to learn songs efficiently and enhance your overall musicianship.

Understanding Chord Charts

Chord charts are a visual representation of the guitar neck, showing where to place your fingers to form chords. They are a fundamental tool for learning new songs and expanding your chord vocabulary.

- **Chart Layout:** A chord chart shows the guitar facing upward, with six vertical lines representing the strings. The left line represents the low E string, and the right represents the high E string.

Horizontal lines will represent the frets, usually consisting of only five at a time, and dots will indicate where your fingers will be placed on the fretboard.

Sometimes (but not always), there will be numbers within the dots to indicate which fingers are used to form the chord.

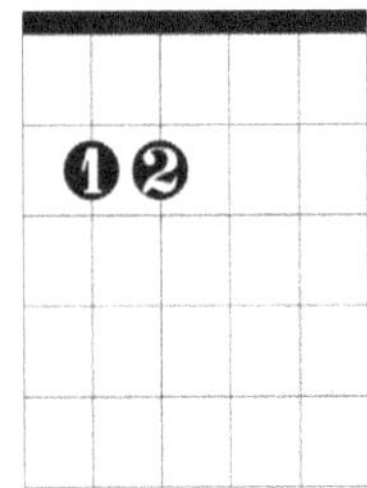

In this example, the first two fingers will be placed on the 6th and fifth strings on the 2nd fret. This will form the E minor chord.

Remember that when reading the chord chart, the guitar is facing upwards, not sideways like it is normally played.

- **Finger Positioning:** Numbers on the dots correspond to the fingers of your fretting hand: 1 for the index finger, 2 for the middle finger, 3 for the ring finger, and 4 for the pinky.

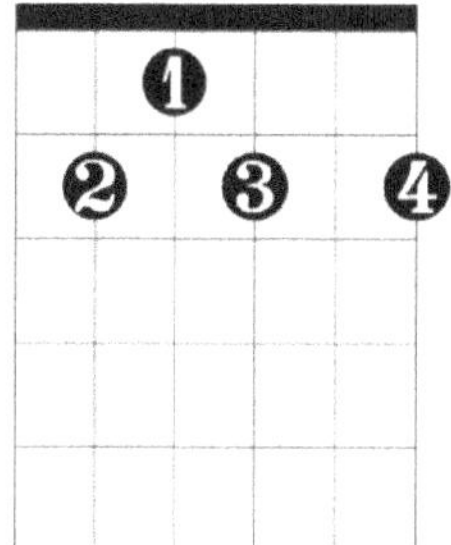

In the example above, all four fingers are used for this chord formation. 1st finger is on the 4th string first fret, 2nd finger on the 5th string second fret, 3rd finger on the 3rd string second fret, and the 4th finger on the 1st string second fret.

This arrangement forms the B7 chord. Another very popular chord found in many songs.

By studying and reading chord charts, you'll be able to learn songs more quickly and develop a better understanding of how music is written.

Interpreting Scale Diagrams

Scale diagrams provide detailed visual guides for various guitar scales and positions along the fretboard, offering a deeper understanding of how to execute them more proficiently.

- **Scale Diagrams**: These diagrams map out the notes of a particular scale across the fretboard. Each dot represents a note, and diagrams often show the root note in a different color or shape.

Unlike the chord chart that faces upward, a scale diagram faces sideways. With the dark part to the left representing the nut. Some scale diagrams won't have that. Just as the chord chart, the diagram consists of vertical and horizontal lines.

In this case, though, since it is facing sideways, the horizontal lines will be the guitar strings (the low E on the bottom), and the vertical lines will represent the frets.

Guitar notation with string names

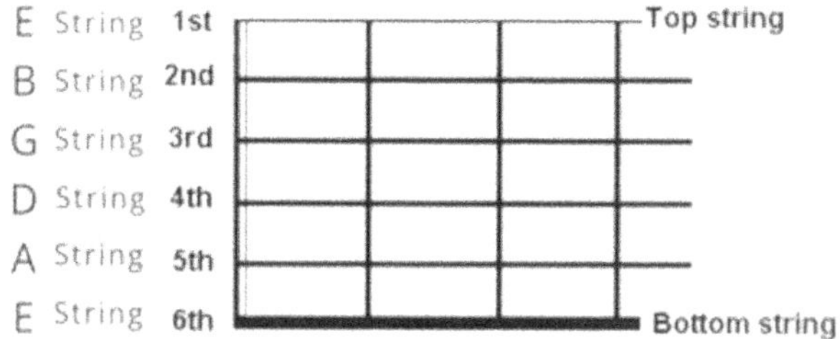

The thing that is tricky about guitar notation is the fact that the lowest string (your biggest on the top of your guitar) is on the bottom. This is because the lowest note in standard sheet music is always at the bottom.

Tab is no different, so make sure that you remember this. It will make it a lot easier to read. Study the picture above to fully grasp this concept.

Scale Diagram Indicating a Scale

Once you fully understand the diagram, it's a matter of looking at it with a scale included. Once again, it will be very similar to the chord chart, except it'll be facing sideways and have more notes.

The C Major Scale: C D E F G A B

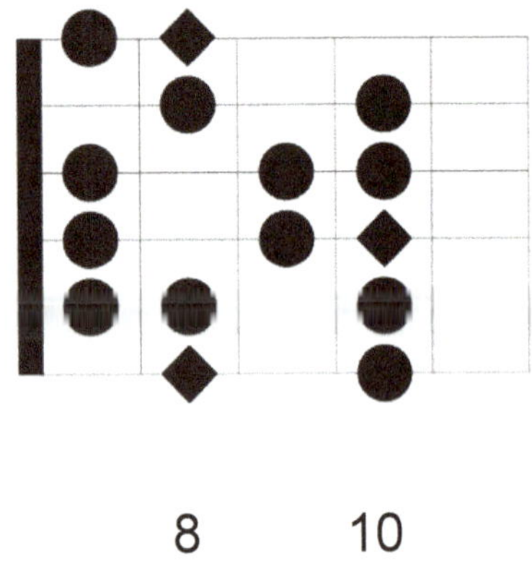

The diamond shapes indicate the root of the scale, and you can see that it is in three locations within the scale. This scale is played at the 8th fret, where the C note is located.

The A Natural Minor Scale: A B C D E F G

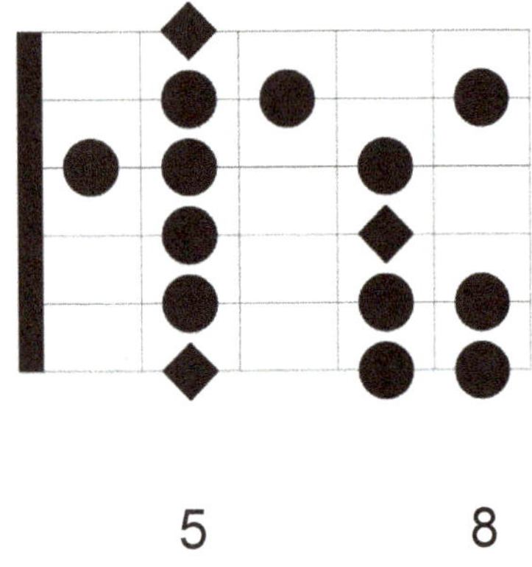

This will be played at the 5th fret, where the A note is located.

Lesson 8: Reading Guitar Tabs

Guitar tablature, or tabs, is a simplified form of musical notation that is widely used by guitarists to learn songs quickly and accurately. Mastering tab reading is essential for any guitarist looking to expand their repertoire and improve their playing.

- **Tab Layout**: Tabs consist of six horizontal lines representing the guitar strings, with the top line corresponding to the high E string and the bottom line to the low E string. Numbers on these lines indicate which fret to press down.

In this example, you have six horizontal lines that represent the six guitar strings, with the low E on the bottom. Vertical lines are not usually used to separate frets; only measures are separated.

- **Reading Tabs:** Each number corresponds to a fret on a particular string. Since there are six strings, there might be multiple numbers.

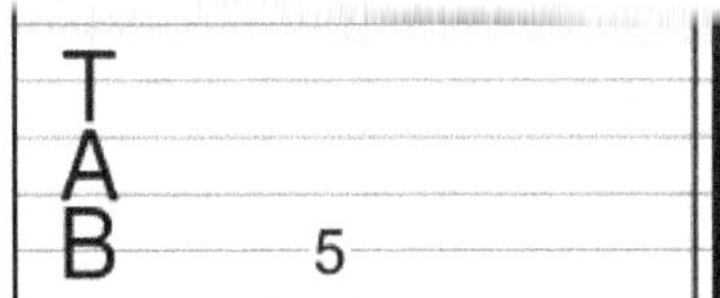

In this example, you place your finger at the 5th fret on the 5th string.

In this example, you play multiple notes. First at the 5th fret, and 8th fret on the 6th string, followed by the 5th and 7th fret on the 5th string. Four notes that are played one after the other.

In addition to numbers, you will also encounter such things as chords and lead guitar techniques. Chords will be numbers stacked on top of each other when played together.

Chords Written in Tabs

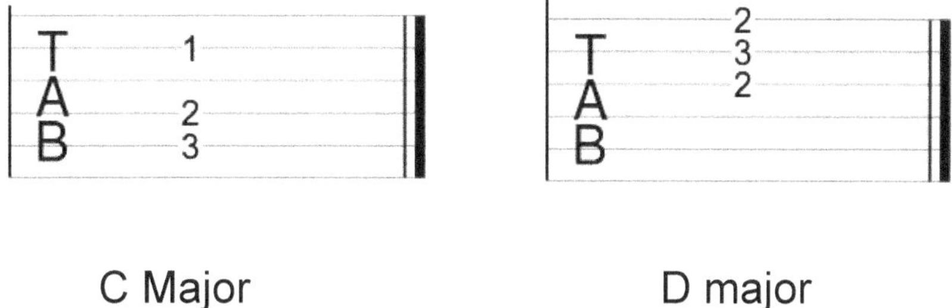

       C Major   D major

These chords indicate that the notes are played together, as if you were strumming them.

When the notes of the chords are played individually, the notes are written in a slant order, not stacked on top of each other.

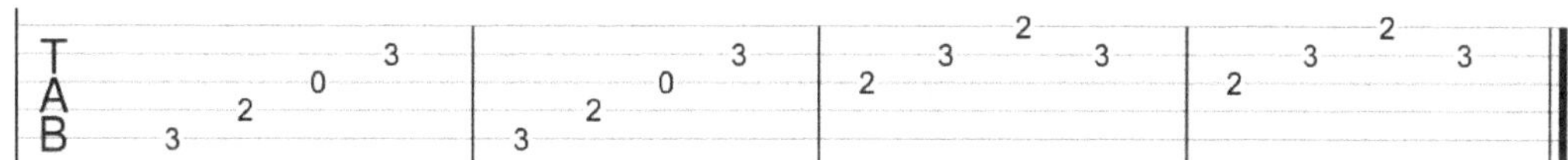

In this example, the chords are the same, C major and D major. They are written at a slant to indicate the notes are played individually.

Playing chords in this fashion is called arpeggiating chords, or playing arpeggios. For now, just grasp the basic understanding of tabs, how they are written, and how to read them.

Techniques for Practicing with Tabs

Once you are familiar with the basics of reading tabs, developing effective practice strategies will help you learn songs more efficiently.

- **Start Simple:** Begin with simple songs or riffs that use basic chords and patterns.

This approach helps you become comfortable with reading tabs and translating them to the fretboard.

- **Break It Down**: Divide the song into sections and focus on mastering each part individually before piecing them together.

This method prevents you from becoming overwhelmed and allows for more focused practice.

- **Listen and Play Along:** Listen to the song while playing along with the tabs. This practice reinforces your understanding of timing and rhythm.

By mastering the skill of reading guitar tabs, you open up a world of musical possibilities to learn a variety of songs.

Lesson 9: Guitar Riffs

Guitar riffs are an essential skill for any lead guitarist, as riffs often form the backbone of a song. This lesson will guide you through understanding and playing guitar riffs, with practical examples to enhance your skills.

Understanding Guitar Riffs

Guitar riffs are short, catchy musical phrases that are repeated throughout a song. They are often used in rock, blues, and pop music to create memorable hooks.

- **Defining a Riff**: A riff is typically a repeated sequence of notes or chords that establishes the main theme or feel of a song. Riffs can be simple or complex, but their primary purpose is to capture the listener's attention.

This is an example of a simple guitar riff played on the low E string.

- **Identifying Riffs in Music**: Listen to various songs to identify their riffs. Pay attention to the rhythm, melody, and repetition that characterize each riff. Understanding these elements will help you recognize and learn riffs more efficiently.

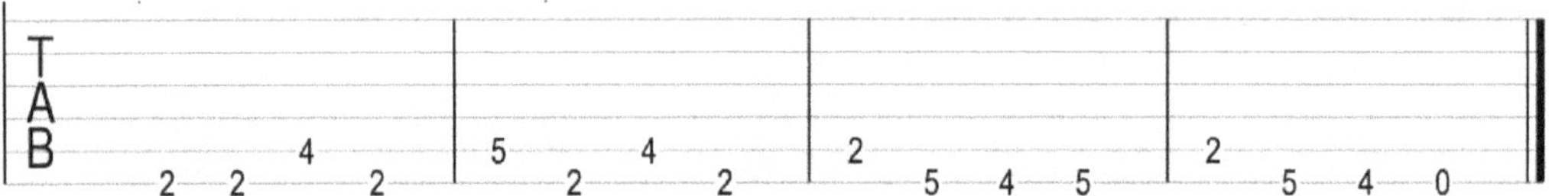

Here is an example of a simple guitar riff played over two strings. In this example, you want to use the 2nd fret on the 6th string as a pivot note. Notice how the beginning of the riff keeps coming back to it.

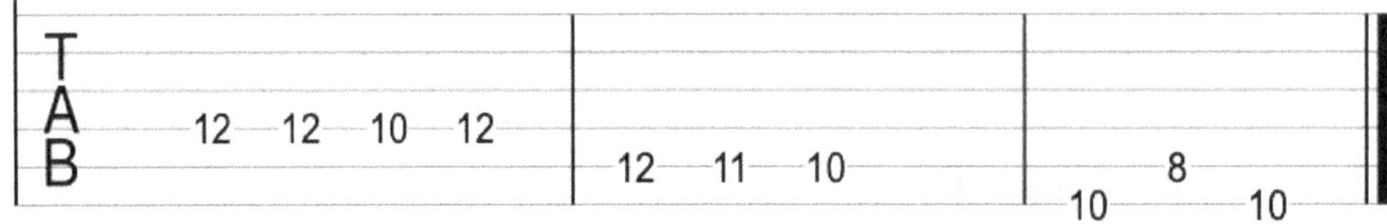

Here is an example of a simple guitar riff played over three strings. This is a nice one because it lets you play further up the fretboard.

Tips For Practicing Riffs

Practicing guitar riffs with tabs helps you focus on finger placement and rhythm so you can play them accurately and confidently.

- **Break It Down:** Divide the riff into smaller, manageable sections. Focus on mastering each part individually before piecing them together.

This approach prevents you from becoming overwhelmed and allows you to focus on challenging sections.

- **Focus on Timing and Groove:** Pay close attention to the timing and groove of the riff. Practice playing along with a metronome or backing track to develop a strong sense of rhythm.

This is especially important for riffs with syncopated or off-beat timing elements to their rhythm.

- **Slow It Down:** Begin practicing riffs at a slower tempo to ensure accuracy in finger placement and picking technique.

Use a metronome to maintain a steady rhythm and gradually increase the speed as you become more comfortable with the riff.

- **Use Proper Technique**: Ensure that you are using the correct picking and fretting techniques for the riff.

Pay attention to alternate picking, palm muting, and finger placement to achieve a clean, articulate sound.

- **Experiment with Variations**: Once you have mastered the riff, experiment with variations by changing the rhythm, adding embellishments, or altering the dynamics. This exploration can help you develop your creativity and personal style.

By following these tips, you'll be able to practice guitar riffs effectively, leading to improved technique, timing, and musicality. This skill will not only enhance your ability to play riffs accurately but also enrich your overall guitar playing and creative expression.

Chapter III Quiz

In Chapter 3, you have learned about reading diagrams, tablature, and guitar riffs. All are designed to enhance your musicianship by helping you read guitar notation.

Q: What do the lines represent in a chord chart?

A: ____

Q: What do the dots on a chord chart represent?

A: ____

Q: What does a number on a tab line signify in guitar tabs?

A: ____

Q: How are reading guitar tabs different from chord charts?

A: ____

Q: What is the key characteristic of a guitar riff?

A: ____

Q: What techniques are important when learning guitar riffs?

A: ____

Chapter III summary

First, you learn about reading chord charts. These are box diagrams that represent chords. With vertical lines indicating the strings, horizontal lines indicating the first five frets, and dots indicating where you place your fingers.

Second, you learn about reading scale diagrams. These are designed for reading scales. Whereas chord charts face upwards, these face sideways and indicate where notes are located in a scale box pattern.

Third, you learn about reading tablature, which is called tabs for short. These are another type of sheet music for stringed instruments, using numbers to indicate which fret is pressed down on the fretboard.

Fourth, you learn about reading guitar riffs. Guitar riffs are an essential skill for any lead guitarist, as riffs often form the backbone of a song. Guitar riffs are short pieces of music that are easily recognizable.

Lastly, by mastering reading guitar notation, including chord charts, scale diagrams, tablature, and guitar riffs. You enhance your ability to learn songs faster and expand your repertoire.

Chapter IV: Lead Guitar Techniques

Lesson 10: Hammer-ons and Pull-offs

Hammer-ons and pull-offs are essential techniques for any lead guitarist looking to add fluidity and speed to their playing. These techniques allow for smooth transitions between notes and are commonly used in solos and melodic phrases.

Mastering Hammer-ons

Hammer-ons involve striking a note on a higher fret using the finger without picking the string again. This technique creates a smooth, legato sound and is crucial for playing fast, fluid passages.

- **Basic Technique**: Begin by picking a note on the guitar, then use a finger on your fretting hand to press down on a higher fret without re-picking the string. Ensure the hammer-on is quick and decisive to produce a clear sound.

- **Practice Exercises:** Start with simple exercises on one string, such as moving from the 5th fret to the 7th fret. Gradually increase speed and incorporate hammer-ons into scale patterns to develop proficiency.

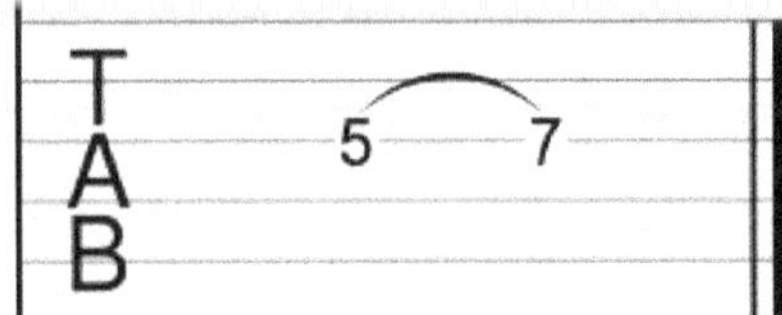

A hammer-on in tablature is indicated by an arc between two notes. In this example, you have a hammer-on from the 5th fret to the 7th fret on the 3rd string. Pick the 5th fret, and then hammer-on to the 7th without picking it.

This technique allows you to play two notes while picking only one. This creates a nice fluid motion among the notes.

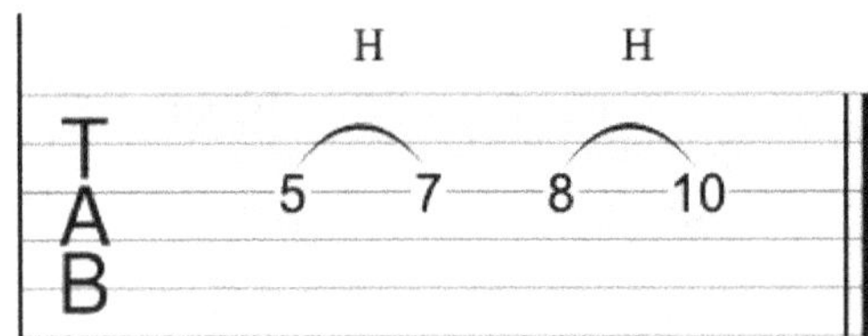

In this example, you have two hammer-ons played one after the other. Both on the 3rd string. One from 5 to 7, and the other from 8 to 10. Work on playing these all over the fretboard.

Developing Pull-offs

Pull-offs are the counterpart to hammer-ons and involve pulling the finger off a higher fret to a lower one, producing a note without re-picking the string.

- **Basic Technique**: Start by playing a note on a higher fret, then "pull" the finger off the string to sound a note on a lower fret, which is already fretted or open. Ensure the pulling motion is smooth and controlled to maintain note clarity.

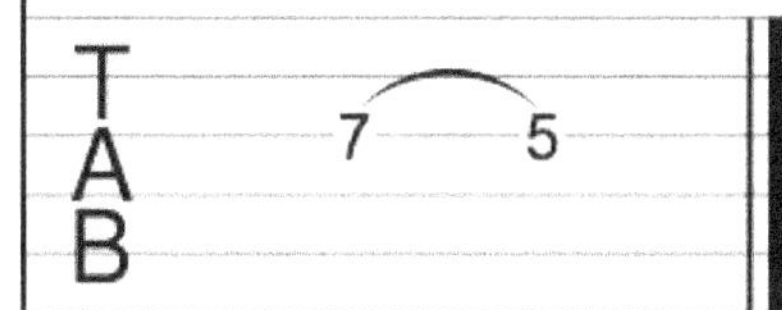

As you can see, this is written in tab in the same fashion as the hammer-on. The only difference is the notes. Since you are pulling off instead of hammering on, you will have a larger number in front.

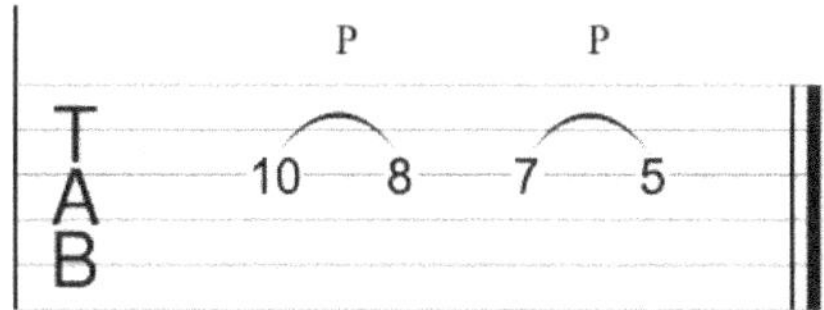

48

As you can see, the pull-off is the opposite of the hammer-on.
Think of them like adding and subtracting. A hammer-on adds
a note, and a pull-off subtracts a note.

The only difference is that with a hammer-on, you put one finger
down and hammer with the other. But with a pull-off, you need
to have two fingers down (unless you're going to pull-off to an
open note) so that when you pick the note, you can pull-off to
the one behind it.

Fluidity in Motion

Hammer-ons and pull-offs are an excellent way to create fluidity
in motion. They let you play more notes with less picking effort
since only one of the two notes is picked.

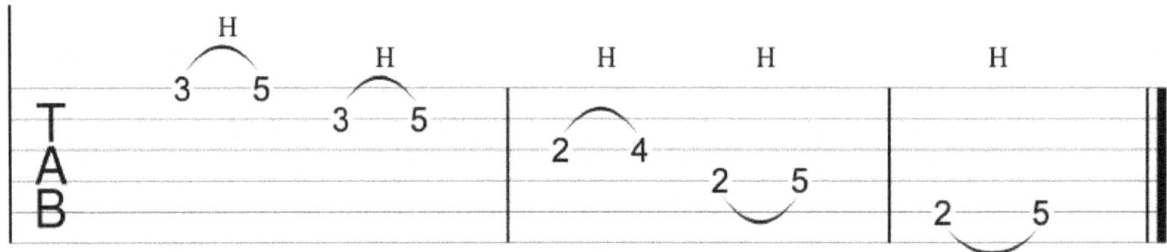

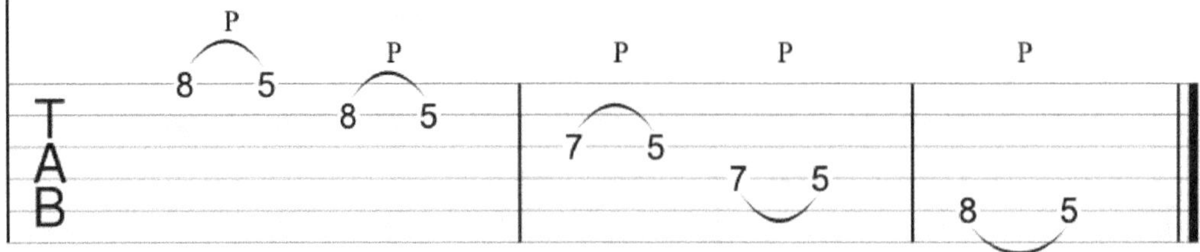

Hammer-ons and Pull-offs Together

Individually, these two techniques can create nice fluid note sequences, but together they are even more effective. Make sure to learn them individually, then work at playing them together.

- **Combining Techniques:** Practice sequences that alternate between hammer-ons and pull-offs, such as trills. This will enhance your finger strength and agility, allowing for more dynamic and expressive playing.

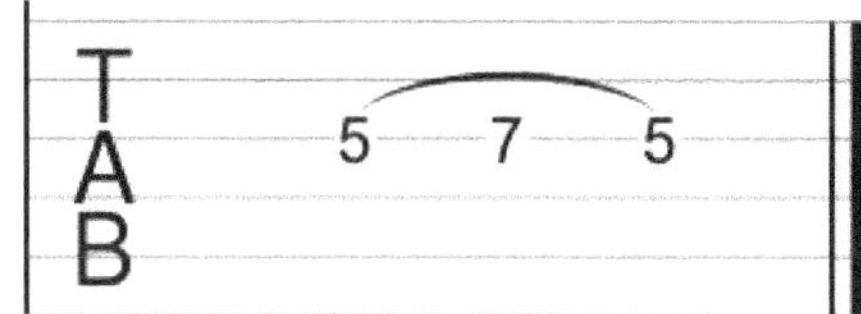

When you combine the two techniques, it will be written as an arc over three notes. In this example, you hammer-on from the 5th fret to the 7th, then pull-off back to the 5th, all on the 3rd string.

When you combine the two techniques, you can play three notes with only one pick. This creates a nice fluid motion.

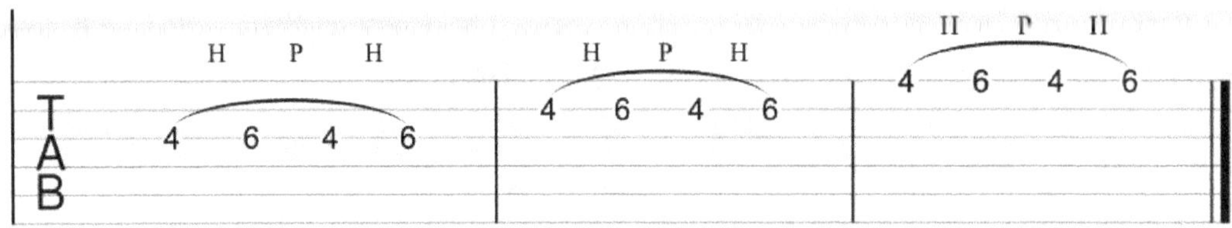

Here is an example of the hammer-on pull-off being played together. You hammer-on on the 6th fret, and then pull off back to the 4th. All in one fluid motion. You repeat this lick on the 3rd, 2nd, and 1st strings.

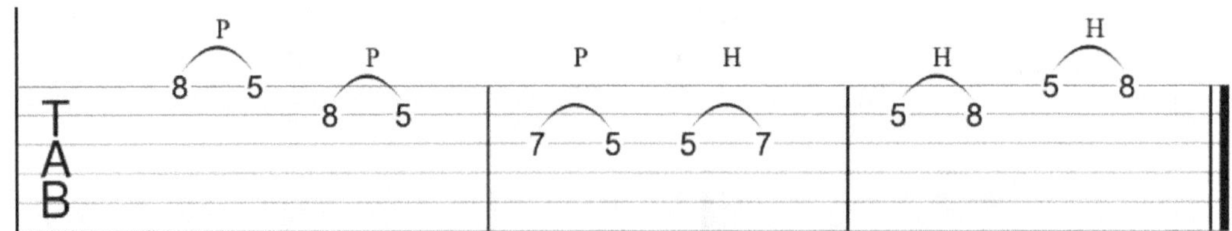

In this example, you start with pull-offs and then reverse the role with hammer-ons. Start on the 1st string, proceed to the 3rd, and then move back to the 1st string.

By mastering hammer-ons and pull-offs, you can add a new level of expressiveness to your guitar playing, enabling you to execute intricate lead passages with ease and fluidity.

Lesson 11: Bends, Slides, and Vibrato

Incorporating bends, slides, and vibrato into your playing will significantly enhance your expressiveness as a lead guitarist. These techniques add emotion and character to solos, allowing you to convey a wide range of feelings through your music.

Mastering Bends and Slides

Bends and slides are crucial techniques that add fluidity and emotion to your lead guitar playing. Understanding and mastering these techniques will help you create seamless and expressive musical phrases.

- **Bends**: Bending involves pushing or pulling a string across the fretboard to raise the pitch of a note. Begin by practicing half-step and whole-step bends, ensuring you reach the target pitch accurately.

Use your wrist for leverage, and keep other fingers on the string for support. Listening for pitch accuracy is essential, as bends should match the intended note precisely.

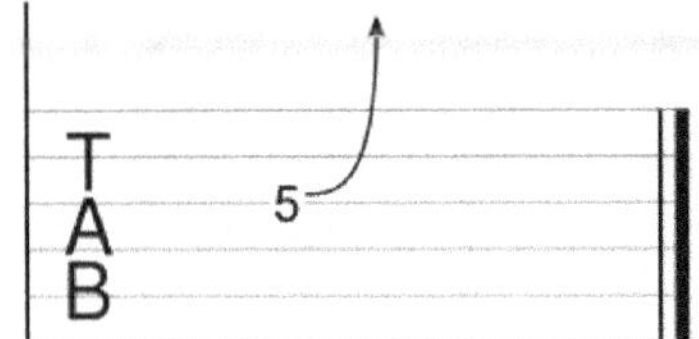

A string bend written in tab is indicated by an arc going upward toward the ceiling. String bends can be in different pitches, usually a half step (one fret) or a whole step (two frets), and can be released as well.

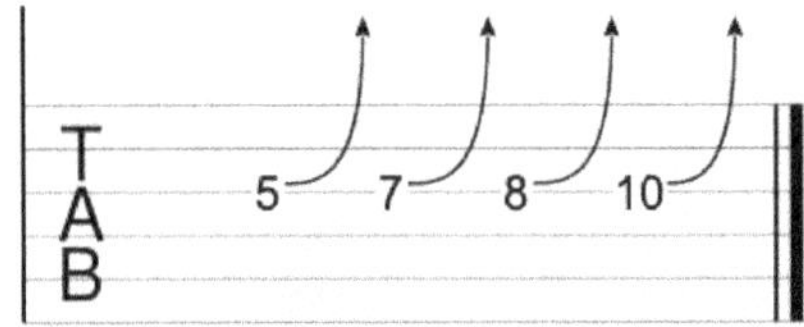

In this example, you have four individual string bends that move up the fretboard on the 3rd string. Pick the note, and then push it up.

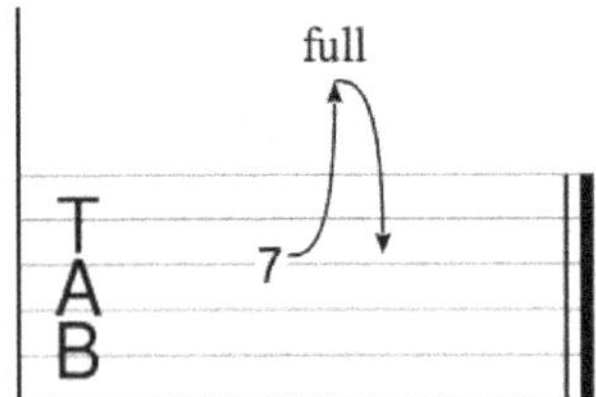

In this example, you bend the note and then release it.

Slides

- **Slides:** Sliding allows you to smoothly transition between notes without re-picking the string. Start by playing a note and maintaining pressure as you slide your finger up or down the fretboard to a new note.

Slides written in tab are indicated by a slanted line between two notes. One direction is going up, and the opposite going down.

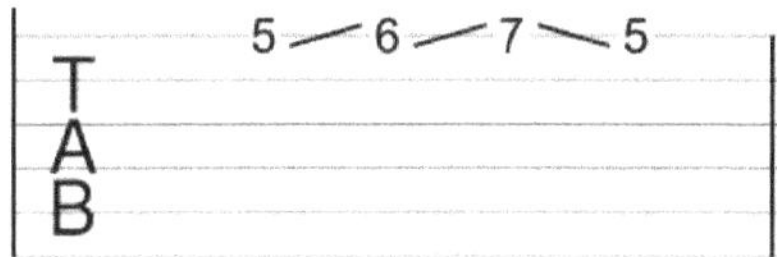

In this example, you pick the 5th fret and slide up to the 6th and 7th frets, then slide back down to the 5th fret. All on the 1st string.

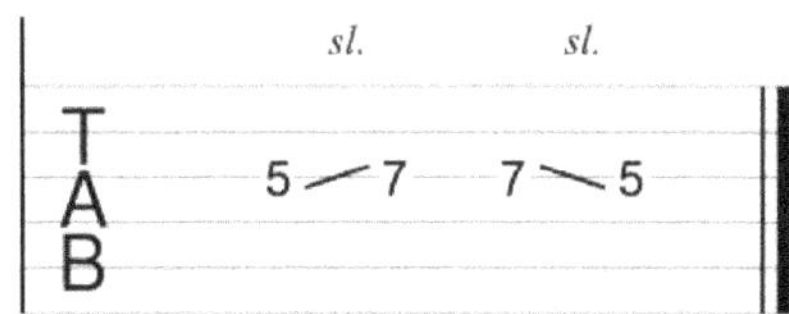

In this example, you slide up from the 5th to the 7th fret, and then slide down from the 7th back to the 5th, all on the 3rd string.

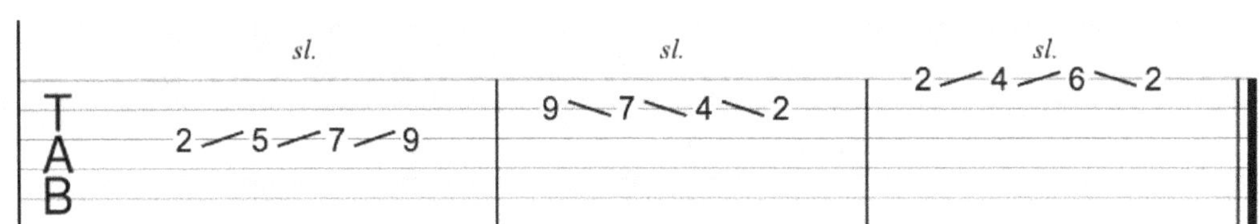

In this example, you practice sliding up and down from the 2nd up to the 9th on the 3rd, 2nd, and 1st strings.

Slides are also thought of as ascending and descending, which is sliding up and sliding down. For easier learning, I just call it sliding up and down.

Sliding From Note To Note

The objective in well-designed slides is to accomplish sliding to the correct fret. This can be a bit challenging when sliding further distances along the fretboard.

- **Slide Up:** Press the string down, hold it, and slide up to another fret.

Make sure to keep your finger firmly in place when moving over the fret wire, as this will hinder the sound.

- **Slide Down:** The same thing goes for sliding in the opposite direction. Keep your finger firmly pressed along the fretboard for maximum efficiency.

When sliding up and down the fretboard, make sure to focus on which fret you are sliding to. Start with a short distance, like one or two frets, and gradually increase the length.

Developing Vibrato Technique

Vibrato adds depth and emotion to your playing by subtly varying the pitch of a note. This technique is essential for creating a rich, expressive sound that can transform a simple note into a captivating musical statement.

- **Basic Vibrato**: Begin by playing a note and moving your fretting finger back and forth perpendicular to the fretboard. The motion should be controlled and consistent, with the wrist providing the movement.

Vibrato is indicated in the tab by a wavy line above the note.

In this example, you pick the 7th fret on the 3rd string and slightly push the note up and down to create a vibrating effect.

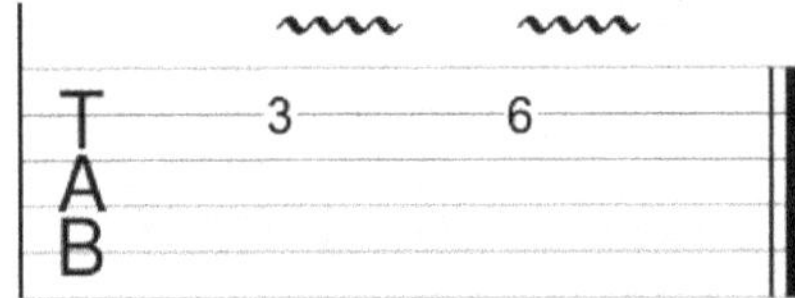

In this example, you vibrate two notes one after the other. First at the 3rd, and then at the 6th. Both on the 2nd string.

- **Practicing Vibrato**: Incorporate vibrato into your practice routine by applying it to sustained notes in scales and solos. Focus on maintaining a steady rhythm and controlled movement.

By mastering bends, slides, and vibrato, you'll be able to add a new level of expressiveness to your guitar playing.

Lesson 12: Trills, Harmonics, and Tremolo Picking

In this lesson, we will explore three additional techniques that can add flair and excitement to your lead guitar playing: trills, harmonics, and tremolo picking.

These techniques provide unique ways to express musical ideas and can enhance your solos with their distinct sounds.

Mastering Trills and Harmonics

Trills and harmonics are techniques that add texture and variety to your playing. Understanding and mastering them will allow you to incorporate new sounds and techniques into your guitar repertoire.

- **Trills**: A trill is a rapid alternation between two adjacent notes. To play a trill, use a hammer-on and pull-off motion between the two notes.

Start slowly to ensure clarity and gradually increase speed. Practice trills on different strings and frets to develop finger strength and agility. Incorporating trills into your solos can add excitement and urgency.

Trills written in tab are indicated by a "tr" with a wavy line above the note. The note that it is hammered on to will be smaller in parentheses. This can be executed in half or whole steps.

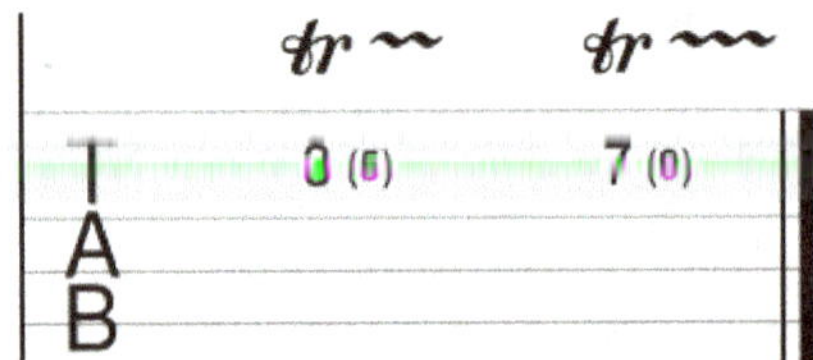

In this example, you play a trill at the 3rd fret to the 5th, and then one at the 7th fret to the 9th. These are done individually, one after the other, and executed on the 2nd string.

Here is an example of trills played in the same fashion, but on different frets moving up the fretboard. All on the 3rd string, starting at the 2nd fret and moving up to the 7th.

Trills are a great way to build finger strength.

Harmonics

Harmonics are bell-like tones produced by lightly touching a string at certain points, called nodes, while plucking it. There are two main types of harmonics: natural and artificial.

- **Natural Harmonics:** These are played by lightly touching the string directly above the 5th, 7th, or 12th fret, then plucking the string. Practice producing clear harmonics by experimenting with finger pressure and position.

Natural harmonics are indicated in the tab by arrows on the outside of each note.

In this example, you have a natural harmonic on the 5th, 7th, and 12th frets. Moving from the 3rd string to the 1st, and back to the 2nd.

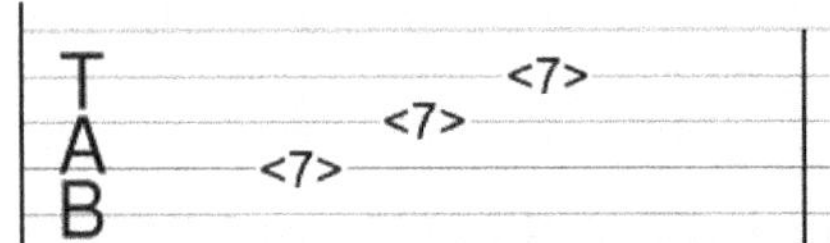

In this example, you play harmonics on the 7th fret only and move from the 4th string to the 2nd.

Remember, when playing harmonics, you don't want to press down on the string like you normally would between the fret wires; you want to lightly touch it right above the fret.

- **Artificial Harmonics:** These require fretting a note, picking it, and then lightly rubbing the string with your thumb afterwards. This harmonic is based on the picking hand, whereas the natural harmonic is based on the fretboard hand.

These are indicated in the tab by an "AH" above the notes to let you know these are artificial harmonics. Remember, these will take some time to master, so be prepared to develop patience.

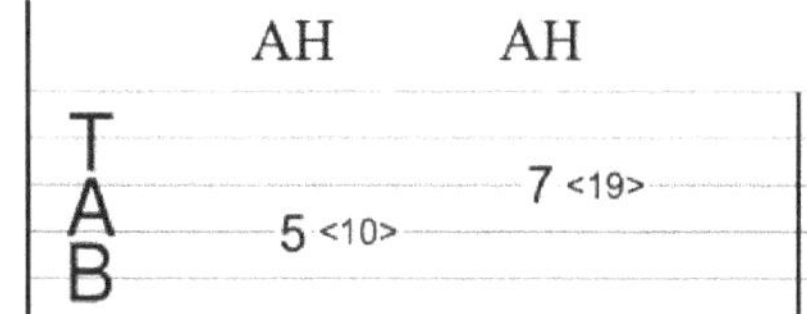

In this example, you play the harmonic at the 5th fret on the 4th string, then at the 7th fret on the 3rd string.

Remember, this type of technique is produced with your picking hand, just like a lot of other techniques in guitar playing. Make sure to put time into developing your picking hand.

Artificial harmonics are not easy to produce, and that is what makes them so special. If you have patience and give them time to develop, you'll be able to make some really cool sounds with them, especially when you add the whammy bar.

Developing Tremolo Picking Technique

Tremolo picking is a rapid picking technique that creates a continuous, fast-paced sound. This technique is widely used in various genres, from classical to metal, and is essential for creating sustained, dramatic passages.

- **Basic Technique**: Tremolo picking is just alternate picking in double time. Focus on using your wrist for the picking motion, keeping the movement relaxed to prevent fatigue, and move quickly.

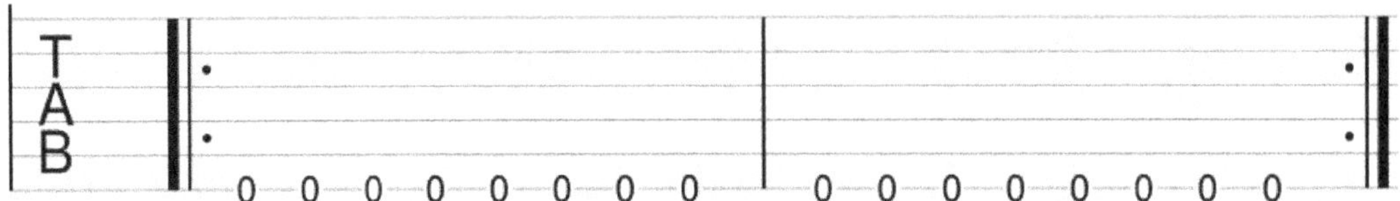

In this example, you pick the open 6th string up and down throughout the measures. This will help you to develop the technique.

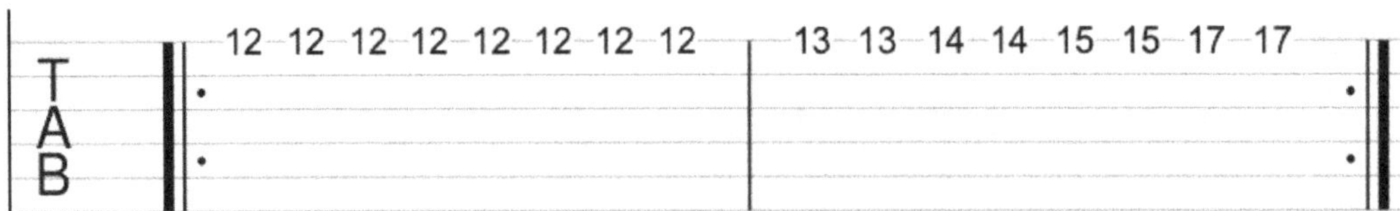

In this example, you do the same thing at the 12th fret, moving up to the 17th fret, all on the 1st string.

By mastering trills, harmonics, and tremolo picking, you'll enrich your lead guitar skills and open up new possibilities for creative expression, textures, and dynamic elements.

Chapter IV Quiz

In Chapter 4, you have learned about hammer-ons, pull-offs, bends, slides, vibrato, etc. These techniques are designed to create melodic musical landscapes.

Q: What is the benefit of a hammer-on in playing lead guitar?

A: ____

Q: How can pull-offs enhance your lead guitar playing?

A: ____

Q: What is the primary goal of using bends in guitar solos?

A: ____

Q: What is the benefit of using vibrato in your guitar solos?

A: ____

Q: What are the two types of harmonics used in guitar solos?

A: ____

Q: What makes tremolo picking so beneficial to your solos?

A: ____

Chapter IV Summary

<u>First</u>, you learn about hammer-ons and pull-offs. These are techniques commonly used by lead guitarists. They are found in almost all guitar solos. They allow you to add fluidity in your phrasing.

<u>Second</u>, hammer-ons are where you pick a note and hammer-on to another note without picking it. A pull-off is the opposite. You have two notes pressed down, you pick the higher note, and pull-off to the lower one.

<u>Third</u>, you learn about bends, slides, and vibrato. Incorporating bends, slides, and vibrato into your playing will significantly enhance your expressiveness as a lead guitarist. These techniques add emotion and character to your solos.

<u>Fourth</u>, you learn about trills, harmonics, and tremolo picking. Three additional techniques that create immense expression. Understanding and mastering them will allow you to incorporate new sounds and techniques into your guitar repertoire.

<u>Lastly</u>, by practicing patience, persistence, and discipline in developing these techniques, you will expand your range of expression and creativity.

Chapter V: Building Finger Dexterity

Lesson 13: Finger Exercises

Developing finger dexterity is crucial for any lead guitarist aiming to play fluidly and with precision.

This lesson will focus on exercises that will strengthen your fingers, increase flexibility, and improve coordination across the fretboard.

Building Finger Strength

Building finger strength is the foundation for achieving speed and accuracy in your playing. By keeping your fingers and hands in shape, you'll be able to execute more complex musical passages.

These exercises target the muscles in your hands and fingers, enhancing your ability to press down on the strings and move quickly between notes.

- **Chromatic Exercise:** Start by playing each fret on a single string, using one finger per fret. For example, on the high E string, use your index finger on the 5th fret, middle finger on the 6th fret, ring finger on the 7th fret, and pinky on the 8th fret.

Move up and back down all six strings, focusing on even timing and clean note production. This exercise improves finger strength and independence.

```
              5   6   7   8
T  |                         |  5   6   7   8      |                    |
A  |                         |                    |   5   6   7   8    |
B  |                         |                    |                    |
```

In this example, you start at the 5th fret on the 1st string and progress to the next four frets. Repeat this exercise on all six strings back and forth.

- **Spider Walk:** Position your fingers on four consecutive frets on any string. Lift and move one finger at a time to the next string, keeping the other fingers in place.

This type of exercise resembles a spider walking and helps develop finger independence and control.

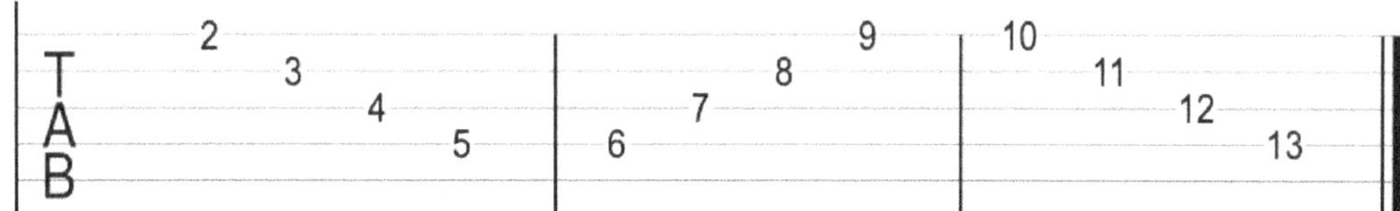

In this example, you spider walk across the strings using all four fingers, starting at the 2nd fret of the 1st string. As you do this, move up the fretboard.

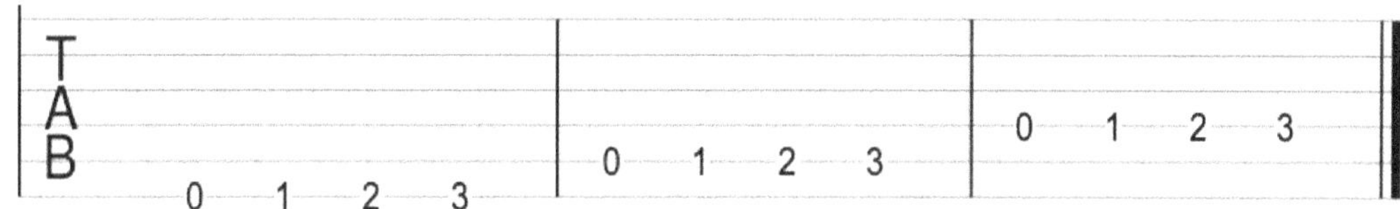

This exercise is similar to the first one, except you start in the open position (without putting a finger on a fret) and progress forward across all the strings.

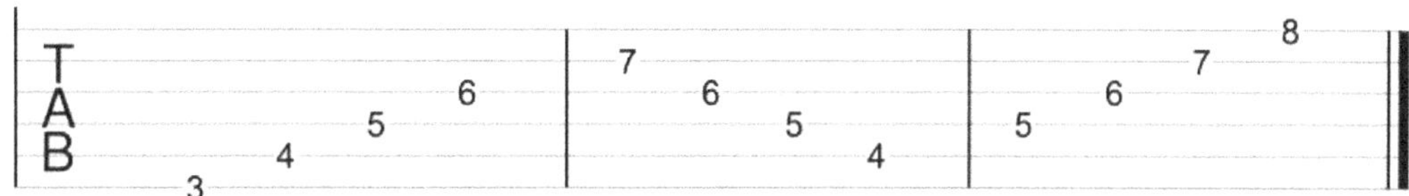

In this example, you do another spider-type walk across the strings. Start on the 6th string and work your way across the fretboard.

Enhancing Finger Coordination and Flexibility

Once you have a strong foundation, focusing on coordination and flexibility will help you navigate complex passages with ease. These exercises are designed to improve your finger agility and ensure smooth transitions across the fretboard.

- **Finger Twisters:** This exercise involves playing sequences that require non-linear finger movements.

For example, play the 1st and 4th frets with your index and pinky, then the 2nd and 3rd frets with your middle and ring fingers. Practice these sequences in different positions and strings to enhance coordination.

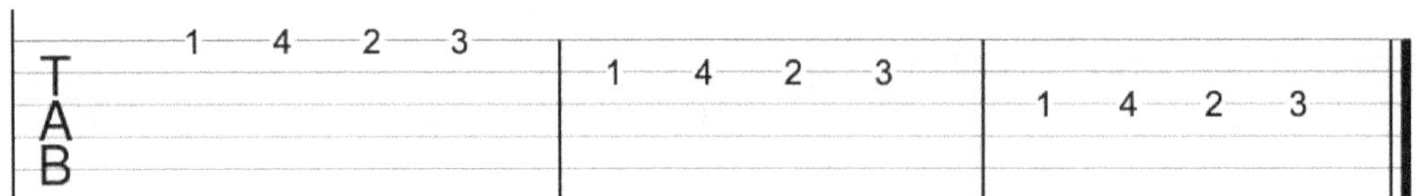

In this exercise, you start on the 1st fret of the 1st string and alternate your fingers. As you do so, you will see that it jars your memory, because it doesn't go in order. This will make playing it fun and challenging.

Lesson 14: Exercising Arpeggios

Arpeggios are when you play the notes of a chord individually. They are an essential tool for any lead guitarist, allowing you to create melodic lines that emphasize the harmony of a song.

Understanding Arpeggios

Playing the notes of a chord in sequence, rather than simultaneously, can be fundamental to constructing solos and adding depth to your guitar playing.

- **Definition and Purpose**: An arpeggio involves playing the individual notes of a chord one after the other.

This technique allows you to outline the harmonic structure of a song while adding melodic interest.

Strumming a chord is a great way to play it, but when you add arpeggios, you can enhance both your rhythm and your lead guitar playing.

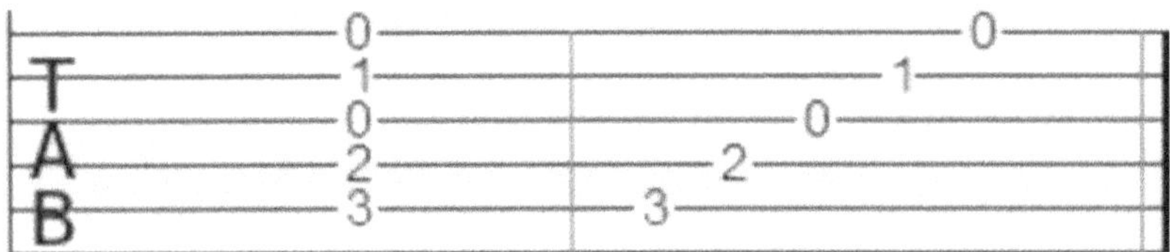

In this example, you have a C major chord written in tab. When the notes are stacked on top of each other, they are played together as in strumming the chord. When they are played individually, such as in an arpeggio, they are written at a slant.

- **Chord Construction:** Understanding how chords are built is key to playing arpeggios. A basic triad consists of three notes: the root, third, and fifth.

For example, a C major chord is made up of the notes C, E, and G. Knowing these components enables you to play arpeggios in various positions on the fretboard.

Practicing Arpeggios on Guitar

Developing the ability to play arpeggios smoothly and accurately is crucial for incorporating them into your solos and improvisations. This topic will guide you through practical exercises to master arpeggios.

- **Basic Arpeggio Patterns:** Start with simple major and minor arpeggio shapes. Practice these patterns across different strings and positions, focusing on clean note production and even timing.

Begin with the open position arpeggios, such as E minor and C major, then move on to other chord-based shapes.

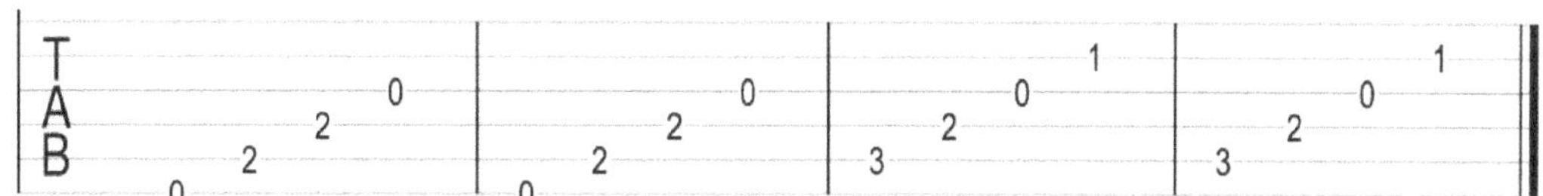

In this example, you arpeggiate the E minor chord for two measures, and then the C major chord.

When arpeggiating chords, make sure to play on the tips of your fingers. This will help to produce a clean, clear sound.

- **Incorporating Arpeggios into Solos:** Use arpeggios to create melodic lines that highlight chord changes in your solos. Practice integrating arpeggios into familiar chord progressions, such as the I-IV-V progression.

Begin by outlining the chords with arpeggios, then add embellishments like slides, hammer-ons, and pull-offs to enhance your phrasing.

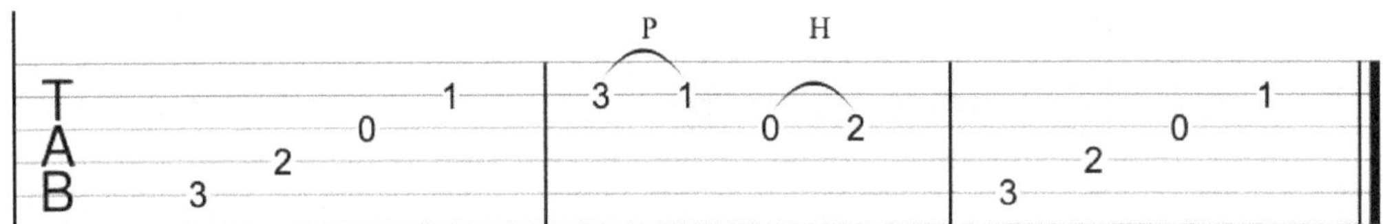

In this example, you arpeggiate the C major chord, and then do a pull-off and hammer-on, finishing off with another C major arpeggio.

Remember, arpeggios can be a great way to enhance your finger dexterity. By playing chords in this way, you add diversity to your lead guitar playing as well as improve your picking technique.

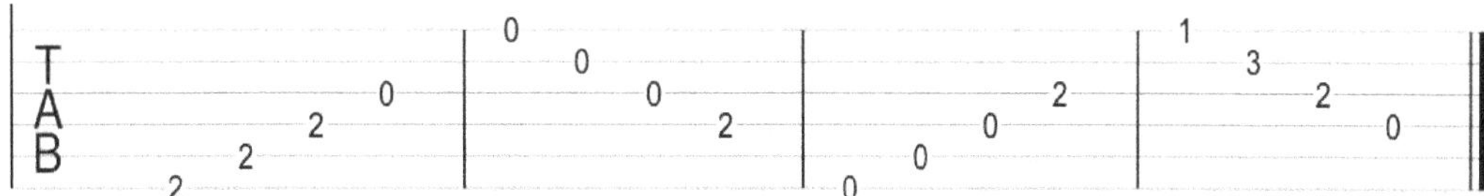

Here is another arpeggio example that improves finger dexterity.

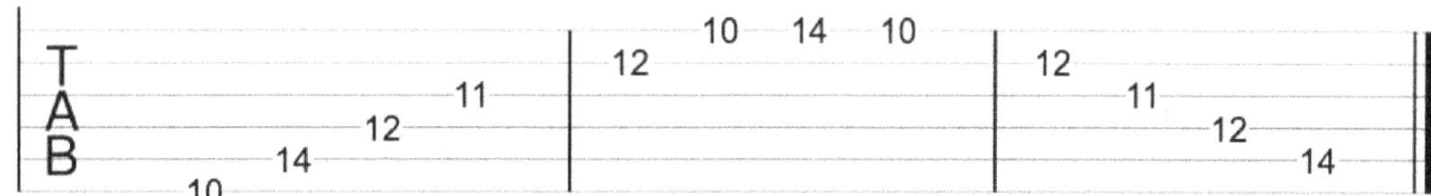

In this arpeggiated example, you start at the 10th fret on the 6th string and work your way up to the 14th fret on the 1st string. Giving you an option to play further up the fretboard.

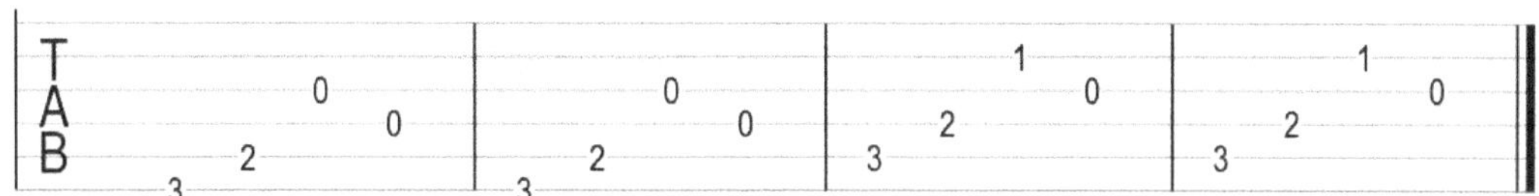

In this example, you arpeggiate the G major chord for two measures, then arpeggiate the C major chord for two measures. Notice how the C major chord is different from the one previously presented.

Applying Arpeggios in Improvisation

Once you've become comfortable with the basic shapes and execution of chord arpeggios, the next step is to apply them creatively in your lead guitar playing.

This topic will guide you through integrating arpeggios into your solos and compositions, enhancing your ability to craft cohesive, engaging musical narratives.

- **Emphasizing Chord Tones:** Use arpeggios to highlight the chord tones within a progression. This creates a strong melodic connection to the harmony, making your solos sound more intentional and harmonically rich.

Practice improvising over a simple chord progression, focusing on using arpeggios to outline each chord change. Begin by emphasizing the root, third, and fifth of each chord, then experiment with adding extensions like the seventh or ninth for more color.

By integrating arpeggios into your improvisation, you'll add depth and sophistication to your solos, creating more expressive, harmonically interesting music.

Lesson 15: String Skipping

String skipping is an advanced technique that adds a new dimension to your lead guitar playing by allowing you to create wide intervals and unique melodic lines.

Mastering this technique will enhance your ability to play complex solos with precision and flair.

Understanding String Skipping

String skipping involves playing notes on non-adjacent strings, creating a distinct sound that is often used to add complexity and interest to solos. This technique requires precise picking and fretting, as it involves larger hand movements and coordination.

- **Definition and Purpose**: String skipping allows you to bypass one or more strings between notes, creating wide intervals that can make your solos stand out.

It is commonly used in rock, metal, and fusion genres to add a dynamic, modern edge to performances.

- **Basic Technique:** Start by practicing simple exercises that involve skipping one string, such as playing a note on the 6th string, then a note on the 4th.

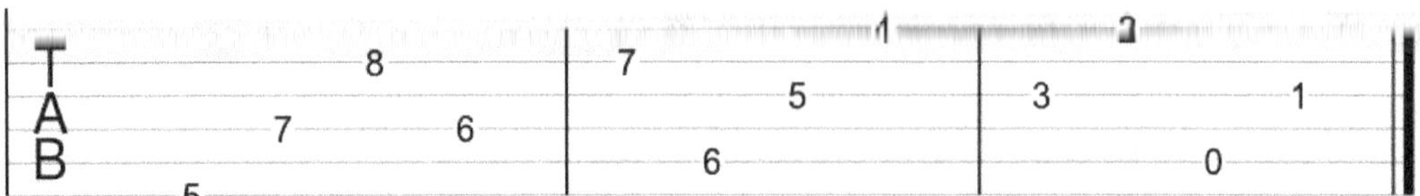

In this example, you play the 5th fret on the 6th string and skip to the 7th fret of the 4th string, and so forth.

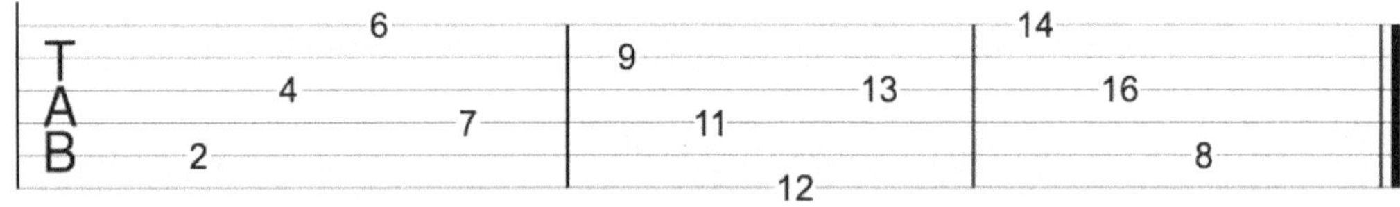

In this example, you start at the 2nd fret on the 5th string and skip to the 4th fret on the 3rd string and so forth. Notice how you progress all the way up to the 16th fret.

This technique is an excellent way to develop finger dexterity while creating interesting runs for your lead guitar playing.

More String Skipping Exercises

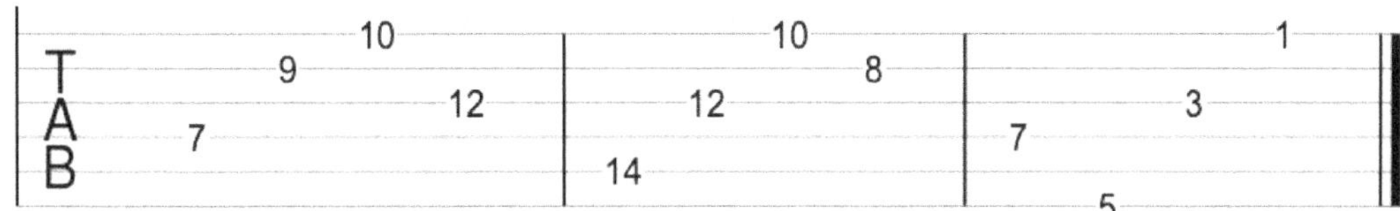

In this example, you start at the 7th fret on the 4th string, skip to the 9th fret on the 2nd string, and so forth.

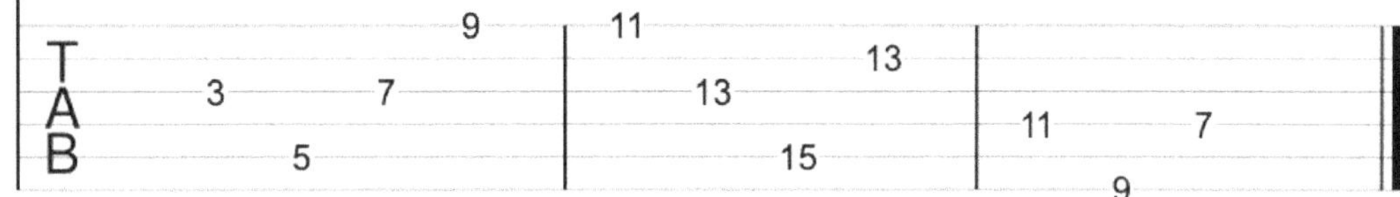

In this example, you start at the 3rd fret on the 3rd string, skip to the 5th fret on the 5th string, and so forth.

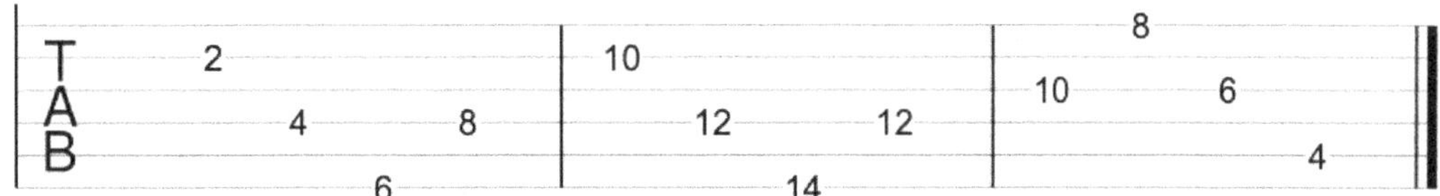

In this example, you start at the 2nd fret on the 2nd string, skip to the 4th fret on the 4th string, and so forth.

Remember, these exercises are a great way to build dexterity.

Practicing String Skipping Patterns

Developing proficiency in string skipping requires dedicated practice and attention to detail. This topic will guide you through exercises and strategies to master this challenging technique.

- **String Skipping Exercises:** Begin with exercises that focus on common string skipping patterns.

  Gradually incorporate more strings as you become comfortable with the technique.

- **Incorporating String Skipping into Solos:** Practice integrating string skipping into your solos by using it in familiar scale patterns and arpeggios. For example, use string skipping to play a C major arpeggio by skipping strings between notes to create a more expansive sound.

Experiment with combining string skipping with other techniques, such as hammer-ons, pull-offs, and slides, to develop your unique style.

By mastering string skipping, you'll add an exciting, modern element to your guitar solos and melodies.

Chapter V Quiz

In Chapter 5, you learned about building finger dexterity. Finger exercises, chord arpeggios, and string skipping are all designed to develop maximum playability.

Q: How are chromatic finger exercises beneficial?
A: ____

Q: How are spider-walk finger exercises beneficial?
A: ____

Q: How are arpeggios beneficial to dexterity development?
A: ____

Q: How can arpeggios enhance your guitar solos?
A: ____

Q: What is the primary benefit of string skipping in guitar solos?
A: ____

Q: What is a key technique for enhancing your string skipping?
A: ____

Chapter V Summary

First, you learn about finger exercises. The first step in building finger dexterity. Developing finger dexterity is crucial for any lead guitarist aiming to play fluidly and with precision.

Second, you learn that building finger strength is the foundation for achieving speed and accuracy in your playing. By keeping your fingers and hands in shape, you'll be able to execute more complex musical passages.

Third, you want to exercise arpeggios. Playing the notes of a chord in sequence, rather than simultaneously, can be fundamental to constructing solos and adding depth to your guitar playing.

Fourth, arpeggios give you more control over your picking hand and force you to make sure you are forming your chords with proper finger positioning. If you ever want to know if you are forming your chords correctly, arpeggiate them.

Lastly, you learn how string skipping can also be a good way to enhance not only your finger dexterity, but also your solos. Mastering this technique will enhance your ability to play complex solos with precision and flair.

Chapter VI: The Pentatonic Scales

Lesson 16: The Major Pentatonic Scale

The major pentatonic scale is a versatile and widely used scale in various genres, from rock and blues to jazz and country. Its simple yet effective structure makes it an essential tool for any lead guitarist.

Understanding the Major Pentatonic Scale

To effectively use the major pentatonic scale in your playing, it is crucial to understand its structure and theoretical basis. This knowledge will enable you to apply the scale across different keys and musical contexts.

- **Scale Structure**: The major pentatonic scale consists of five notes derived from the major scale. It omits the 4th and 7th degrees, resulting in a more open and consonant sound.

For example, the C major pentatonic scale includes the notes C, D, E, G, and A.

- **Musical Context:** The major pentatonic scale is often used in solos and improvisations because it fits seamlessly into various chord progressions. Its lack of half steps means it generally avoids dissonance, making it an excellent choice for melodic lines.

C Major: C D E F G A B = 1 2 3 4 5 6 7

C Major Pentatonic: C D E G A = 1 2 3 5 6

G Major: G A B C D E F# = 1 2 3 4 5 6 7

G Major Pentatonic: G A B D E = 1 2 3 5 6

D Major: D E F# G A B C# = 1 2 3 4 5 6 7

D Major Pentatonic: D E F# A B = 1 2 3 5 6

As you can see from these examples, the major pentatonic scale takes five notes out of its major scale. This makes it easier to use.

Understanding its application across different musical styles is key to using the scale effectively over a wide range of chord progressions.

Playing the Major Pentatonic Scale on Guitar

Once you understand the structure of the major pentatonic scale, the next step is to apply it to the guitar fretboard. This topic will guide you through learning the scale patterns and integrating them into your playing.

- **Fretboard Patterns:** Begin by learning the major pentatonic scale in the open position, such as the C major pentatonic scale. Next, explore movable patterns that can be transposed to any key.

Familiarize yourself with these patterns across the fretboard to ensure flexibility in your playing and mastery of the fretboard.

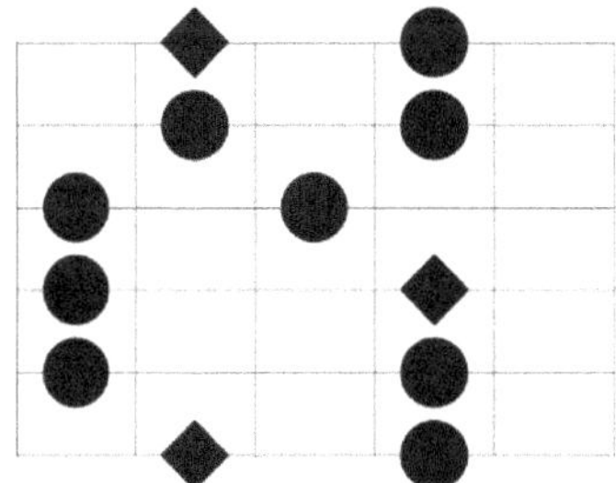

Here is an example of the major pentatonic scale as it lies across the fretboard. Remember, the 6th string is on the bottom, and the diamond symbols are the root notes.

The Major Pentatonic in Different Keys

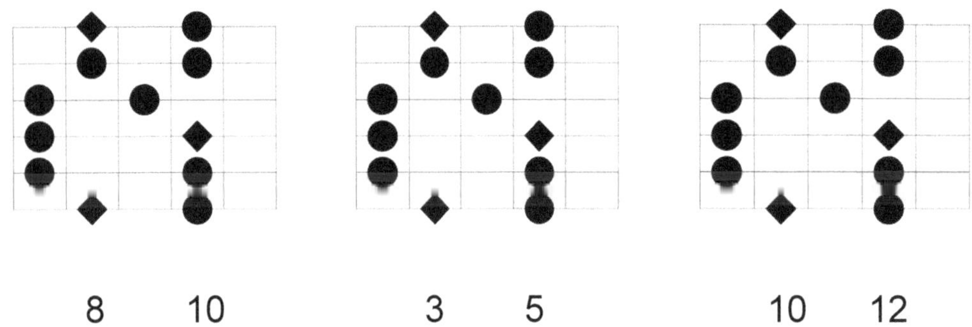

As you can see from these examples, the pattern is the same, but located in different places along the fretboard.

Played at the 8th fret, it is the C major pentatonic scale.

Played at the 3rd fret, it is the G major pentatonic scale.

Played at the 10th fret, it is the D major pentstonic scale.

If you were to play the F sharp major pentatonic scale, you'd play the pattern at the 2nd fret.

By mastering the major pentatonic scale and its application on the guitar, you will expand your musical vocabulary and develop the ability to craft engaging, melodic solos that resonate with your audience.

Lesson 17: The Minor Pentatonic Scale

The minor pentatonic scale is a staple of lead guitar, renowned for its versatility and emotive sound. It's a fundamental scale for improvisation, particularly in blues, rock, and jazz, and the most popular one of them all.

Understanding the Minor Pentatonic Scale

Pentatonic stands for two things. Penta, meaning five, and tonic, meaning notes. Five notes. A scale of five notes.

To harness the power of the minor pentatonic scale, it's essential to understand its construction and theoretical background.

- **Scale Structure**: The minor pentatonic scale consists of five notes derived from the natural minor scale. It omits the 2nd and 6th degrees, which contributes to its distinct, bluesy character. For example, the A minor pentatonic scale includes the notes A, C, D, E, and G.

- **Musical Context:** The minor pentatonic scale is favored for its simplicity and emotive quality. Its lack of half steps minimizes dissonance, making it ideal for improvisation.

Understanding its use across different musical contexts helps you incorporate the scale seamlessly into solos and compositions.

A Minor: A B C D E F G = 1 2 b3 4 5 b6 b7

A Minor Pentatonic: A C D E G = 1 b3 4 5 b7

G Minor: G A Bb C D Eb F = 1 2 b3 4 5 b6 b7

G Minor Pentatonic: G Bb C D F = 1 b3 4 5 b7

D Minor: D E F G A Bb C = 1 2 b3 4 5 b6 b7

D Minor Pentatonic: D F G A C = 1 b3 4 5 b7

As you can see, the minor pentatonic scales work the same way that the major pentatonics do. The only difference is the two notes that are omitted. With the minor, it's the 2nd and the 6th, whereas with the major, it's the 4th and the 7th.

Playing the Minor Pentatonic Scale on Guitar

Once you grasp the theoretical aspects of the minor pentatonic scale, it's crucial to apply it practically on your guitar. This topic will guide you through learning the scale patterns and using them in your playing.

- **Fretboard Patterns**: Begin with the A minor pentatonic scale at the 5th position, then explore movable patterns that can be transposed to any key.

Familiarize yourself with this pattern across the fretboard to ensure versatility in your improvisation.

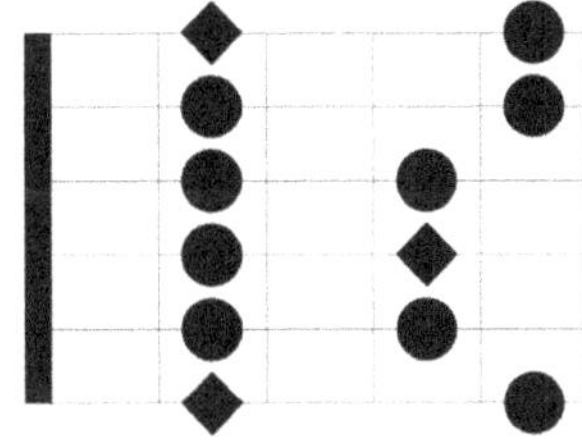

This is the minor pentatonic scale box pattern. Just like the major, but shaped differently. As you can see, the notes line up in a simple, easy-to-play pattern.

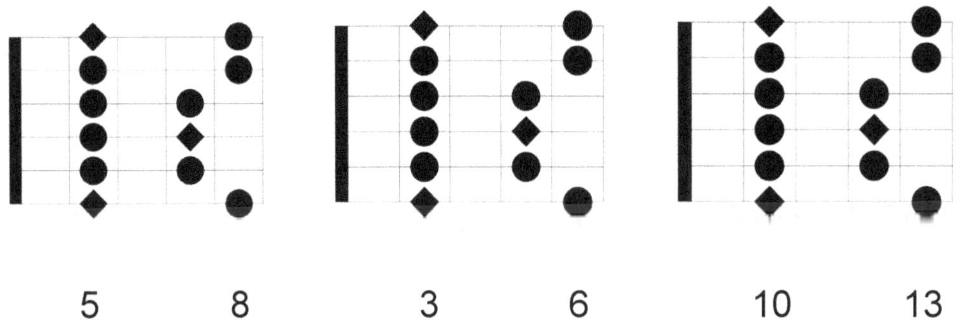

Here we have the minor pentatonic scale in three locations. If it is played at the 5th fret, it is in the key of A minor; if it is played at the 3rd fret, it will be in the key of G minor; and if it is played at the 10th fret, it will be in the key of D minor.

- **All Minor Keys:** This applies to all other minor keys. Find the note along the fretboard, and start the scale pattern there.

Since the notes line up in a pattern, it will be easier to learn them if you can visualize them as a pattern. Patterns and shapes will make it easier to learn most things on the guitar.

Practical Applications of the Minor Pentatonic Scale

The minor pentatonic scale is not only foundational to lead guitar playing but also incredibly versatile. This topic will explore how to effectively integrate the minor pentatonic scale into your solos and compositions, enhancing your musical expression and creativity.

- **Expanding Your Musical Vocabulary**: Use the minor pentatonic scale as a basis for developing new licks and riffs. Incorporate techniques such as bends, slides, and hammer-ons to add expressiveness and variety to your playing.

Practice combining different licks to create longer, cohesive musical phrases that maintain listener interest. This will be learned later in the training.

By mastering the minor pentatonic scale and its application on the guitar, you will significantly expand your ability to express emotion and creativity in your music, making it an indispensable tool in your lead guitar arsenal.

Lesson 18: The Power of Five Patterns

The pentatonic scales, both major and minor, are fundamental to many musical genres. Understanding the versatility and application of these five-note patterns can elevate your improvisation skills and expand your creative possibilities. This lesson will explore how to harness these patterns effectively.

Exploring Five Patterns in Different Positions

The pentatonic scales consist of five distinct positions on the guitar fretboard. Mastering these positions is crucial for fluid navigation across different keys and developing versatility in your playing.

- **Position 1 (Root Position)**: Start with the most common pentatonic shape, often used as the foundation for solos. This position centers on the root note and offers a balanced range of notes for improvisation.

This is the position already presented. Practicing this shape in multiple places along the fretboard helps you understand the scale's ease of structure and tone.

- **Position 2 (Second Position):** This position starts on the second note of the pentatonic scale. It offers a different tonal palette and encourages new melodic ideas.

Practice shifting between the root and second positions to increase your fretboard knowledge and improvisational fluidity.

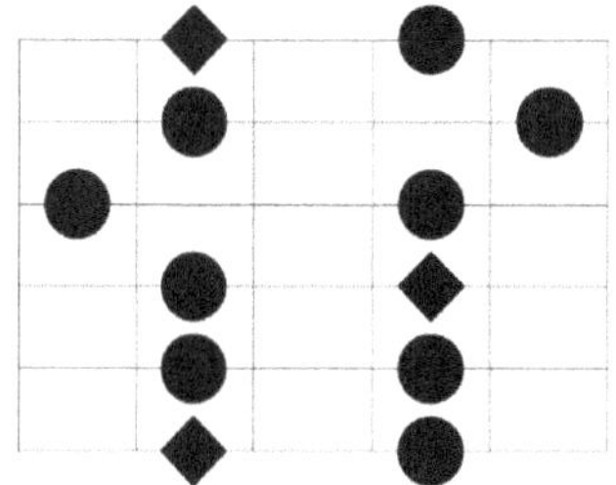

Major Pattern 2

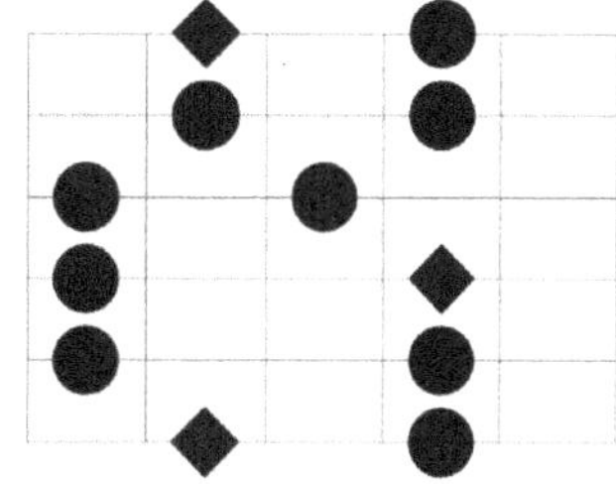

Minor Pattern 2

- **Position 3 (Third Position):** Starting on the third note, this position offers further melodic opportunities. Its unique fingerings can inspire a range of phrasing and articulation techniques. Familiarize yourself with this position to enhance your improvisational versatility.

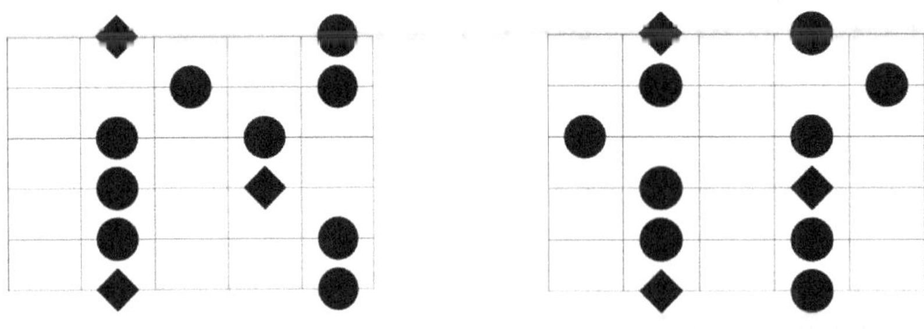

Major Pattern 3   Minor Pattern 3

- **Position 4 (Fourth Position):** Positioned on the fourth note, this shape allows for wide interval jumps and unique melodic lines. Mastering this position helps in creating dynamic solos with expressive phrasing.

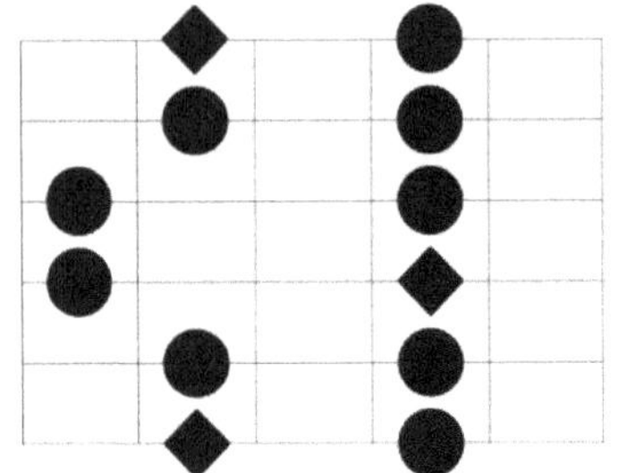

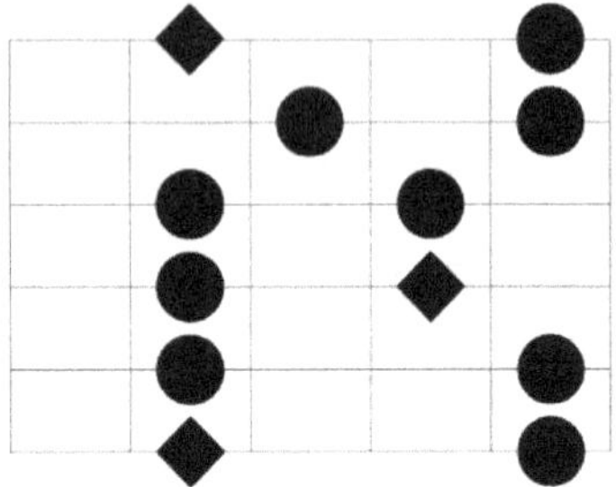

Major Pattern 4   Minor Pattern 4

Remember, all these scale patterns reside on the notes of the scale from which they are derived. For example;

C Major Pentatonic: C D E G A = 1 pattern per note.
A Minor Pentatonic: A C D E G = 1 pattern per note.

- **Position 5 (Fifth Position)**: Beginning on the fifth note, this position completes the cycle of patterns across the fretboard. It provides alternative fingerings and phrasing options, essential for advanced improvisation.

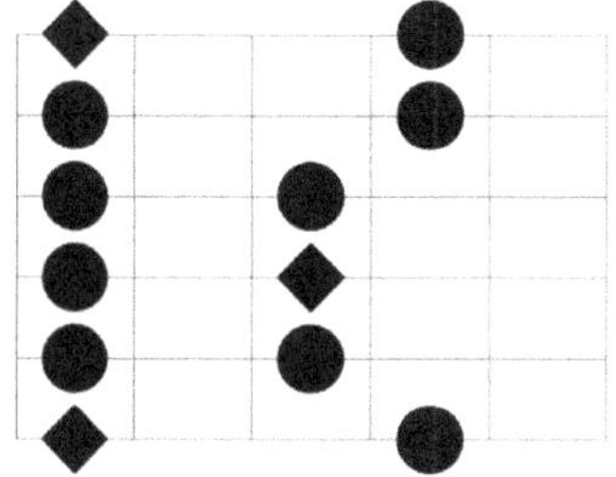

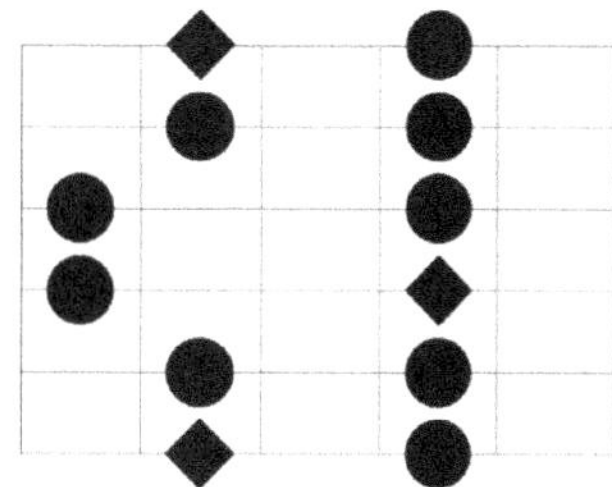

Major Pattern 5   Minor Pattern 5

These are the five pentatonic scale patterns for both major and minor scales. Make sure to study them and know them like the back of your hand. This will give you mastery over the fretboard and enhance your musicianship.

Remember, they will always be in the same order as well, no matter what major or minor key you play them in. The "magical" element of these scales is that the notes line up automatically every time.

As long as you stay in key, you can't go wrong!

Integrating Patterns into Improvisation

Once you understand the five pentatonic patterns, integrating them into your improvisation is essential for developing a comprehensive lead guitar style.

- **Connecting Patterns**: Practice moving smoothly between different pentatonic positions. For instance, start with a lick in the root position, then transition to the second position.

This exercise helps you link patterns and create cohesive solos without getting stuck in one area of the fretboard.

- **Using Patterns in Context**: Apply the pentatonic patterns over various chord progressions, such as the 12-bar blues or rock progressions.

This practice will enhance your ability to adapt your playing to different musical contexts.

By mastering the five pentatonic patterns and learning to integrate them effectively, you'll unlock a new level of improvisational freedom and creativity in your lead guitar playing.

Chapter VI Quiz

In Chapter 6, you have learned about the pentatonic scales. Major, minor, and all five scale patterns. Allowing you to expand your soloing creativity.

Q: What is beneficial about the major pentatonic scale?
A: ____

Q: How many notes make up the major pentatonic scale?
A: ____

Q: What is beneficial about the minor pentatonic scale?
A: ____

Q: Why is the minor pentatonic scale so popular in soloing?
A: ____

Q: Why is the significance of learning all five scale patterns?
A: ____

Q: How can knowing all five help you to enhance your soloing?
A: ____

Chapter VI Summary

<u>First</u>, you learn about the major pentatonic scale. This is where you take five notes out of the seven in the major and create an alternative scale. By doing so, you create a scale that's easier to use and offers more versatility

<u>Second</u>, you learn about the minor pentatonic scale. Like the major, you take five notes out of the seven of the natural minor and create an alternative. This makes it easy to form and use among many different styles.

<u>Third</u>, you learn that with the major pentatonic scale, you omit the fourth and seventh notes. With the minor pentatonic scale, you omit the second and sixth notes. By doing so, you add to your scale vocabulary.

<u>Fourth</u>, you learn that there are five different scale box patterns. Each one is based on a note of the scale. In the key of A minor pentatonic, A, C, D, E, and G, a different pattern would be located at each note interval.

<u>Lastly</u>, the five pentatonic scale patterns in both major and minor will allow you to play solos over any major or minor key. Along with expressing yourself in multiple musical styles, and enhance your mastery over the fretboard.

Chapter VII: Master Improvising

Lesson 19: The 12-Bar Blues Progression

A fundamental element of blues music and a cornerstone for many genres, including rock, jazz, and country, is the 12-bar blues progression.

Understanding this progression is essential for any aspiring lead guitarist, as it provides a versatile framework for improvisation and composition.

Understanding the 12-Bar Blues Structure

The 12-bar blues progression is a repeating chord sequence that forms the backbone of countless blues songs. Its simplicity and adaptability make it an ideal foundation for developing improvisational skills.

This is a great place to start when playing guitar solos. The reason is that this progression is already familiar and works well with lead guitar scales.

- **Chord Structure:** The 12-bar blues progression typically follows the pattern I-IV-V. In the key of G, these chords are G (I), C (IV), and D (V). The basic structure is divided into three four-bar sections:

Bars 1–4: I - I - I - I

Bars 5–8: IV - IV - I - I

Bars 9–12: V - IV - I - V

- **Variations:** While the classic 12-bar blues structure is widely used, musicians often introduce variations to add interest.

Common variations include quick changes (switching to the IV chord in the second bar) and turnarounds (altering the final bar to smoothly transition back to the beginning).

Remember, the 12-bar blues progression is a great place to start, but it's not the only progression you can use with these chords. Any type of rhythm can be created with the I, V, and V chords in any key.

12-Bar Blues Progression

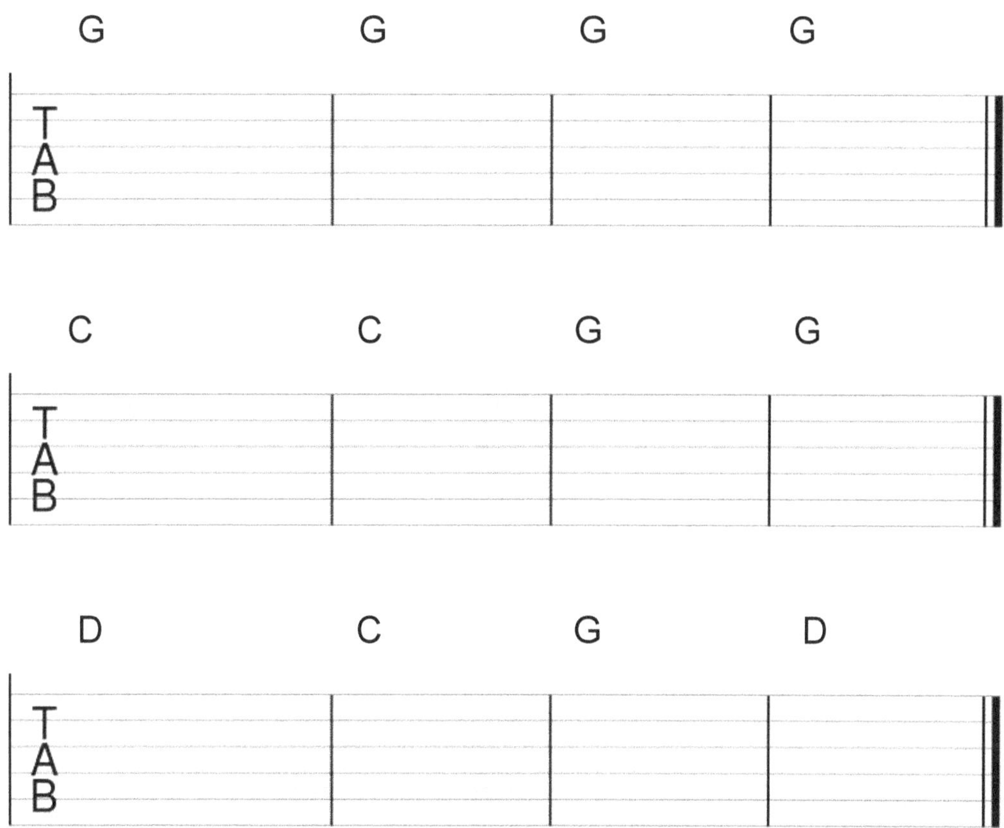

This is the basic fundamental 12-bar progression in the key of G major. Look at the variation suggestions, and try them out to see how they sound.

This is a great progression to start soloing over. Although it's presented in the key of G major, try it out in other keys.

Improvising Over the 12-Bar Blues

Once you understand the structure of the 12-bar blues, the next step is to apply your knowledge by improvising over it. This skill is crucial for creating engaging solos and developing your musical voice.

- **Using the Blues Scale**: The blues scale is a variation of the minor pentatonic scale with an added flat (or "blue note"). In major, this is the flat 3rd note; in minor, it is the flat 5th note.

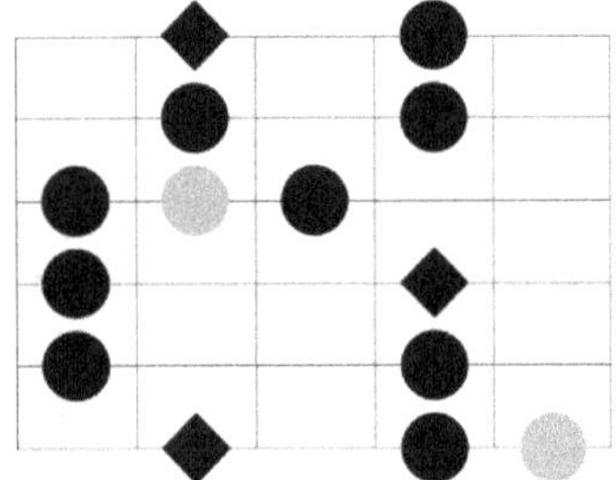
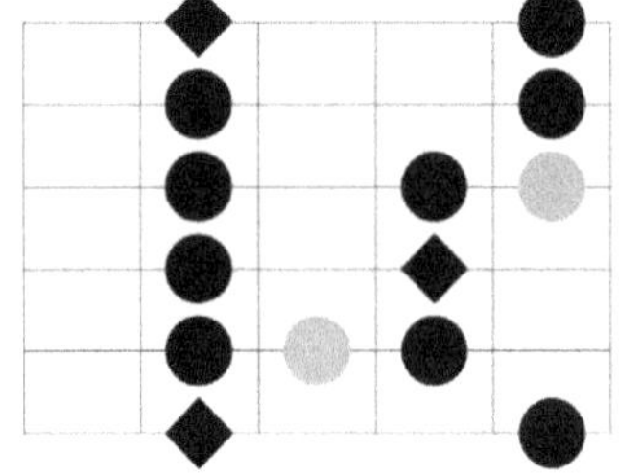

Major Blues Scale   Minor Blues Scale

If you look at these two scales, you'll see that the major adds a flat 3rd note, and the minor has a flat 5th note. These notes are highlighted in blue. Notice how this extends the pentatonic scales, giving you more to create with.

- **Creating Phrasing**: Focus on developing musical phrases that fit the 12-bar structure. Use call-and-response techniques,

where one phrase is followed by an answer, to create a dialogue within your solo. Experiment with repetition and variation to maintain interest and build tension.

- **Incorporating Rhythm**: Rhythm is a key component of blues improvisation. Pay attention to the groove and timing, using syncopation and rests to add dynamics to your playing.

Practice soloing with a metronome or backing track to develop a sense of timing and groove.

By mastering the 12-bar blues progression and learning to improvise over it, you'll gain a deeper understanding of blues music and expand your improvisational skills, paving the way for more advanced musical exploration.

Lesson 20: Phrasing with Guitar Licks

Phrasing is an essential aspect of lead guitar playing that transforms a series of notes into a compelling musical narrative. Developing effective phrasing skills allows you to express emotion and creativity in your solos, making them more engaging and memorable.

Understanding Guitar Licks

Guitar licks are short, expressive musical phrases that serve as building blocks for solos and improvisation. They are often used to convey emotion, highlight musical themes, and create memorable moments in a performance.

- **Definition and Purpose**: A guitar lick is a sequence of notes, often drawn from a scale or mode, used to create a distinct musical idea or motif. Licks can vary in complexity, from simple, catchy phrases to intricate, technical passages. They are essential for adding variety and interest to solos and can be tailored to fit different musical contexts.

Putting it All Together

This is where you get to put all the lessons together that you have previously learned on scales and techniques. The pentatonics, hammer-ons, pull-offs, slides, bends, vibrato, etc.

- **Create Phrasing:** Put techniques together to create phrasing. Very much like an author puts letters together to create words, words together to create sentences, and sentences together to create paragraphs.

These will be the foundation of your guitar solos. Allowing you to give your lead guitar playing a voice to talk and sing.

- **Guitar solos:** These are composed of guitar licks that create phrasing. This is how you bring the scales to life. Playing the scales as notes in a pattern sounds mechanical, but when you add the techniques mentioned in this lesson, it makes them sound like music.

Let's look at some ways we can put guitar licks together to create comprehensive musical landscapes.

Guitar Lick Examples

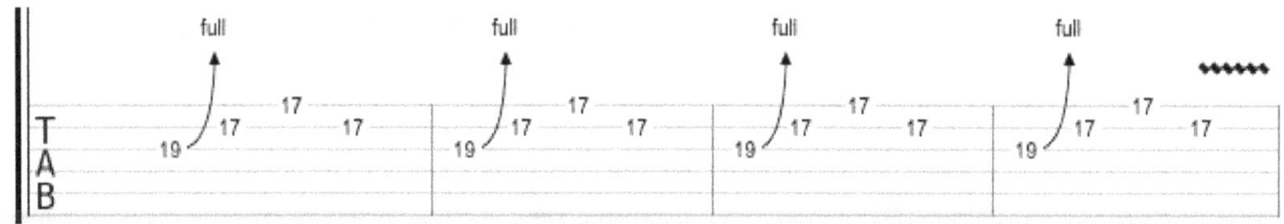

This first example starts with a bend at the 19th fret on the third string, continues with a repeated lick, and ends with vibrato.

In this example, you start with a hammer-on at the 5th fret on the 2nd string, and continue with a four-note repeated lick.

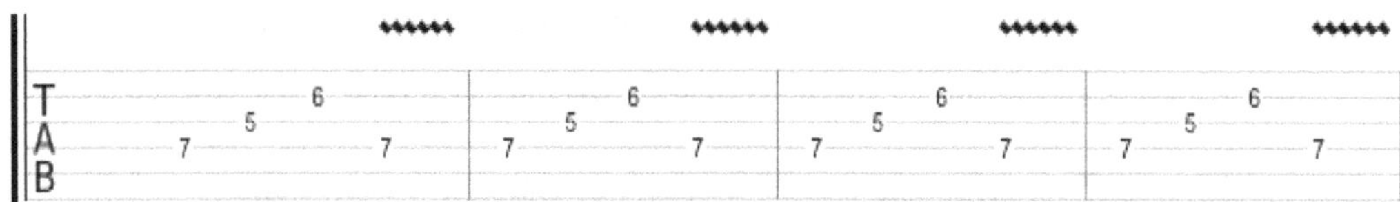

In this example, you start at the 7th fret on the 4th string, you play a simple four-note phrase that repeats and ends with vibrato at the 7th fret on the 4th string.

Notice how these examples utilize techniques you've learned in previous lessons.

Guitar Licks Continued

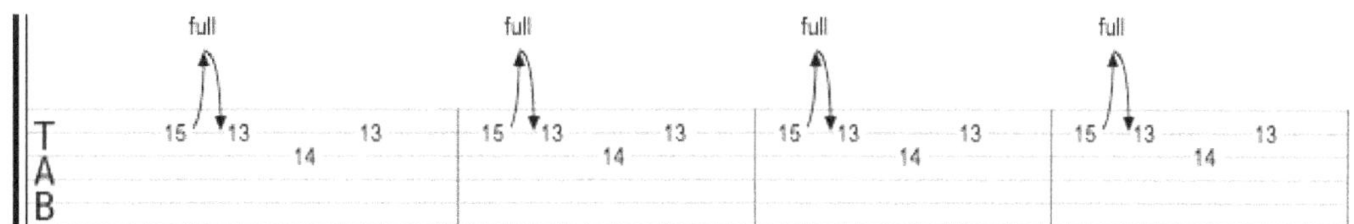

This example starts with a bend release at the 15th fret on the 2nd string, followed by a four-note repeated phrase.

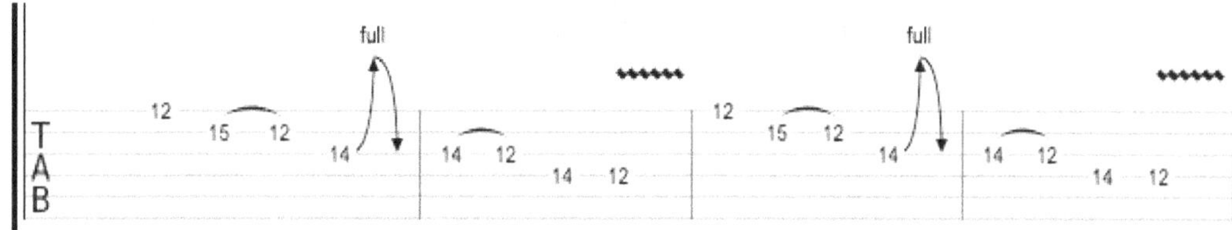

This example uses a pull-off, a bend release, another pull-off, and a vibrato at the end, repeated twice.

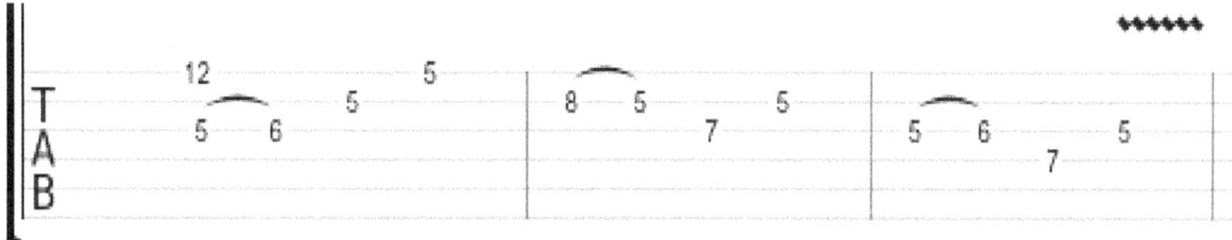

This example starts with a hammer-on at the 5th fret on the 3rd string, adds a pull-off at the 8th fret on the 2nd string, and another hammer-on at the 5th fret on the 3rd string, ending with vibrato.

- **Recognizing Common Licks**: Familiarize yourself with common licks across genres such as blues, rock, and jazz. Listen to recordings of influential guitarists to identify licks that resonate with you.

Understanding these common phrases will help you incorporate them into your playing and develop your unique style.

Developing Phrasing Techniques

Once you understand the role of guitar licks, the next step is to develop techniques for effective phrasing. This involves learning how to articulate notes, control dynamics, and use space to enhance your musical expression.

- **Articulating Notes**: Focus on how each note in a lick is played—whether it's picked, hammered-on, pulled-off, or bent. Experiment with different articulations to add nuance and character to your phrases.

For example, using a bend or slide to transition between notes can add a vocal quality to your playing. See how this is done in the guitar lick examples.

- **Controlling Dynamics:** Dynamics play a crucial role in phrasing, affecting the emotional impact of your music. Practice varying the volume and intensity of your licks, using techniques like palm muting and finger dynamics to create contrast.

This control lets you build and release tension within a solo, keeping listeners engaged.

- **Using Space and Timing:** Effective phrasing involves not only playing notes but also knowing when not to play. Use pauses and rests strategically to create space in your solos, allowing the music to breathe.

Experiment with timing by playing ahead of or behind the beat to add rhythmic variety and interest.

By mastering the art of phrasing with guitar licks, you'll be able to craft solos that captivate your audience and express your musical ideas with clarity and emotion.

Lesson 21: Octaves and Harmony Chords

Understanding octaves and harmony chords is crucial for any lead guitarist seeking to enrich their sound and create more oomplox muoioal arrangomonto.

Mastering Octaves on Guitar

Octaves are a powerful tool for creating a fuller sound and emphasizing melodic lines in your playing. Learning to use octaves effectively can add richness to solos and riffs.

- **Concept of Octaves**: An octave is the interval between one musical pitch and another with double its frequency. On the guitar, this is typically represented by playing the same note on two different strings, usually separated by one or two strings.

Octaves are great for playing solos, riffs, and chords, and, most of all, for mastering the notes' locations on the fretboard.

- **Fretboard Patterns:** To play octaves on the guitar, identify the note you wish to emphasize and find its octave on a different string. A common pattern is to play a note on the 6th string and its octave on the 4th string, two frets up.

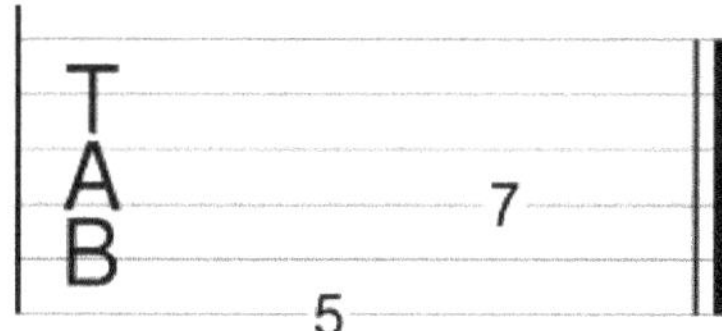

In this example, you have the root 6 octave. An A note at the 5th fret on the 6th string, and an A note on the 7th fret an octave higher on the 4th string.

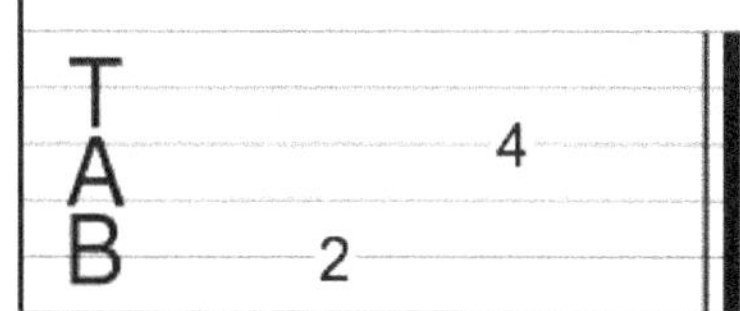

In this example, you have the root 5 octave. Here you have a B note at the 2nd fret on the 5th string, and a B note an octave higher at the 4th fret on the 3rd string.

In this example, you have the root 4 octave. Here, you also have an A note at the 7th fret on the 4th string, and an A note an octave higher at the 10th fret on the 2nd string.

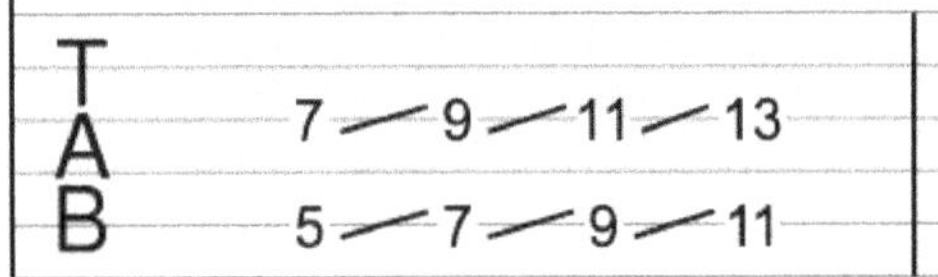

In this example, you have root-5-octave chords. Starting at the 5th fret and sliding up to the 11th fret. These can be used for both soloing and rhythm playing.

- **Applications in Solos and Riffs**: Use octaves to highlight specific notes or phrases in your solos. This technique is often used to create a thicker, more commanding sound.

Incorporate octaves into riffs to add a layer of complexity and power, especially in genres like rock and jazz.

Exploring Harmony Chords

Harmony chords involve playing two or more notes simultaneously to create a harmonious sound. Understanding and using these chords can add depth and texture to your music.

- **Types of Harmony Chords**: Common harmony chords include thirds, fifths, and sixths. These intervals are often used to harmonize melodies or create a fuller sound in chord progressions. For example, playing a melody line in thirds means playing each note a third above it.

Key of C major in 3rds would be the 1 and the 3rd. C and E. Key of A minor in 3rds would be the A and C. The same thing goes for the key of G major in 3rds. G and B.

- **Constructing Harmony Chords**: Start by selecting a melody note and determining the harmony note based on the desired interval. Practice playing these harmony chords in different positions on the fretboard. Experiment with various intervals to explore different harmonic textures.

- **Incorporating Harmony into Playing**: Use harmony chords to enrich your rhythm playing or solos. For instance, in a solo, harmonizing key notes with thirds can add a lush, melodic quality.

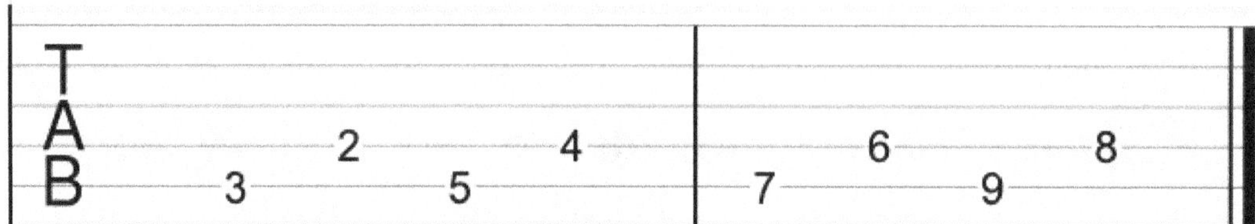

In this example, you play harmony in 3rds. These can be played individually or together as chords.

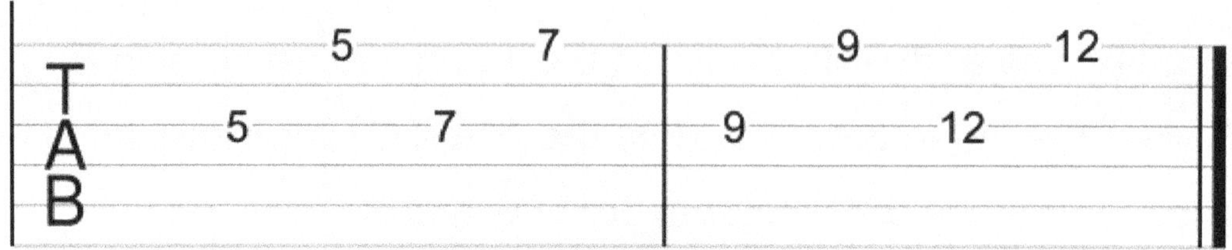

In this example, you have harmony in 6ths. These will be made up of the 1st and 6th of the scale.

Harmonies in fifths are your standard power chords. By mastering octaves and harmony chords, you'll enhance your ability to create complex and engaging musical arrangements.

Chapter VII Quiz

In Chapter 7, you learned how to master improvising by learning the 12-bar blues progression, phrasing with guitar licks, octaves, and harmony chords.

Q: What is the structure of the 12-bar blues progression?

A: ____

Q: What three chords are used in the 12-bar progression?

A: ____

Q: What are guitar licks, and why are they so beneficial?

A: ____

Q: What techniques are commonly used in guitar lick phrasing?

A: ____

Q: How can octaves benefit your mastery of the fretboard?

A: ____

Q: What are the three most common harmony chord types?

A: ____

Chapter VII Summary

First, you learn about the 12-bar blues progression. A fundamental element of blues music and a cornerstone for many genres, including rock, jazz, and country, is the 12-bar blues progression.

Second, you learn that this famous progression is made up of the I, IV, and V of the key it comes out of. For example, if you play the 12-bar blues progression in the key of G major, the chords will be G, C, and D.

Third, you learn about phrasing with guitar licks. This is where you put techniques like hammer-ons and pentatonic scales into play. Phrasing is an essential aspect of lead guitar playing that transforms a series of notes into a compelling musical narrative.

Fourth, you learn about octaves and harmony chords. These are other techniques that can add flavor to your guitar solos. Octaves are also a great way to help you master note locations along the fretboard.

Lastly, Improvising is where you create your own musical voice. With the techniques learned, you start by soloing over the 12-bar blues progression, and progress from there.

Chapter VIII: Additional Training

Lesson 22: Setting Guitar Goals

Setting clear and achievable guitar goals is essential for progressing as a lead guitarist. By defining your objectives, you can focus your practice effectively and track your growth over time.

Defining Short-Term and Long-Term Goals

Understanding the difference between short-term and long-term goals is crucial for creating a structured practice regimen that fosters continuous improvement.

- **Short-Term Goals**: These are specific, attainable objectives that can be achieved in a relatively short time frame, such as a few weeks or months.

Examples include learning a new scale, mastering a difficult riff, or improving your speed in a particular technique. Short-term goals help maintain motivation by providing frequent milestones and a sense of accomplishment.

- **Long-Term Goals:** These goals are broader and more ambitious, often taking months or even years to achieve. They include mastering an entire genre, developing a personal improvisational style, or performing live with confidence.

Long-term goals require ongoing commitment and can be broken down into smaller, manageable tasks to ensure steady progress.

Creating an Actionable Practice Plan

Once you have defined your goals, developing a practice plan is essential for achieving them. This plan should be structured, flexible, and adaptive to your evolving skills and interests.

- **Setting Priorities**: Determine which goals are most important to you and prioritize them in your practice schedule.

Balance your time between technical exercises, theory, and creative exploration to ensure well-rounded development.

- **Tracking Progress:** Keep a practice journal or log to document your activities, achievements, and challenges. Regularly reviewing this record helps identify patterns.

Recognize areas for improvement, and adjust your goals as needed. This reflective practice encourages accountability and continuous growth.

- **Adapting and Evolving:** As you progress, your goals and interests may change. Be open to revisiting and adjusting your objectives to align with your current skills and aspirations. Stay curious and explore new techniques, genres, or collaborations to keep your practice engaging and rewarding.

By setting clear goals and developing a comprehensive practice plan, you'll be well-equipped to pursue your guitar journey with focus and determination, ultimately achieving the mastery and creativity you aspire to as a lead guitarist.

Lesson 23: Developing Practice Habits

Establishing effective practice habits is crucial for any guitarist striving to progress and achieve their musical goals. This lesson will focus on creating a structured practice routine and maintaining motivation to ensure consistent improvement.

Designing an Effective Practice Routine

An effective practice routine is the backbone of your development as a guitarist. It should be tailored to your individual goals, skill level, and available time, ensuring that practice sessions are productive and rewarding.

- **Structuring Your Sessions**: Divide your practice time into focused segments, dedicating specific blocks to different areas such as technique, theory, and creativity.

For example, a 60-minute session might include 20 minutes of warm-up exercises, 20 minutes of scale practice, and 20 minutes of improvisation or learning new songs. This structure helps maintain variety and prevents burnout.

- **Balancing Focus and Flexibility:** While it's important to maintain a structured routine, remain open to adjusting your practice focus as you progress and your interests evolve.

If you find a particular technique challenging, allocate more time to it, or switch to something new if you feel stuck or uninspired. This balance will keep your practice engaging and productive.

Maintaining Motivation and Overcoming Challenges

Staying motivated and overcoming obstacles are essential components of developing lasting practice habits. By fostering a positive mindset and addressing challenges head-on, you can ensure continuous growth in your guitar journey.

- **Setting Short-Term Achievements**: Break down your long-term goals into smaller, achievable milestones. Celebrating these achievements.

Whether it's mastering a new song or improving your speed, it can boost your motivation and provide a sense of accomplishment.

- **Finding Inspiration:** Surround yourself with sources of inspiration, such as listening to your favorite guitarists, attending live performances, or collaborating with other musicians.

These experiences can reignite your passion for guitar and provide new ideas to explore in your practice.

- **Dealing with Plateaus:** It's common to encounter periods where progress seems slow or stagnant. During these times, focus on the aspects of playing that you enjoy most.

Whether it's improvising, composing, or exploring new genres, this shift in focus can help reignite your enthusiasm and provide fresh motivation to continue improving.

- **Growth Mindset:** Adopt a mindset that views challenges as opportunities for growth rather than setbacks, and recognizes that making mistakes and overcoming challenges are all part of the learning process.

Cultivating a Positive Practice Environment

Creating a positive practice environment is essential for maintaining motivation and fostering growth as a guitarist.

Organizing Your Space: Ensure your practice area is tidy, comfortable, and free from distractions. Arrange your equipment—guitar, amplifier, music stand, and any necessary accessories—within easy reach.

A well-organized space allows you to focus on playing rather than searching for items, maximizing your practice time.

- **Creating a Comfortable Atmosphere:** Personalize your practice space to make it inviting and inspiring. Consider adding elements like posters of your favorite musicians, inspirational quotes, or mood lighting. A comfortable, visually appealing environment can boost your mood and increase your willingness to practice.

Develop effective practice habits, maintain motivation, and create a positive practice space to ensure a fulfilling and successful guitar journey.

Lesson 24: Ear Training Proficiency

Developing ear-training proficiency is an essential skill for any guitarist, enabling you to recognize musical elements by ear and enhance your improvisation and composition.

Recognizing Intervals and Chords

Understanding intervals and chords by ear is fundamental for playing by ear, transcribing music, and improving your overall musicality. This topic will guide you through exercises to develop your ability to identify these elements.

- **Interval Recognition**: The distance between two notes, recognized by ear, is crucial for understanding melodies and harmonies. Begin by familiarizing yourself with the sound of common intervals, such as the major third, perfect fifth, and minor sixth.

Practice singing or playing these intervals and relate them to familiar songs that prominently feature them. Use online tools or apps that play intervals for you to identify, gradually increasing the difficulty as you improve.

- **Chord Identification:** Identifying chords by ear is essential for transcribing songs and playing chord progressions on the fly. Start with major and minor chords, focusing on their distinct qualities. Progress to more complex chords, such as sevenths and extended chords.

Listen to songs and try to identify the chords being played, using reference tracks or chord charts as needed. Regular practice will enhance your ability to hear and recognize chords quickly and accurately.

Developing Melodic and Rhythmic Ear

Building a strong melodic and rhythmic ear allows you to transcribe melodies and understand complex rhythms, making you a more versatile and responsive musician. This topic will explore techniques to strengthen these skills.

- **Melodic Transcription:** Practice transcribing simple melodies by ear, starting with nursery rhymes or well-known tunes. Listen carefully to the melody, then try to play it on your guitar.

Focus on getting the pitches and rhythm accurate before moving on to more complex pieces. As you improve, challenge yourself with melodies and diverse styles.

- **Rhythmic Ear Training:** Understanding rhythm is just as important as pitch in music. Practice clapping or tapping along to songs, focusing on the beat and rhythm patterns. Use a metronome to explore different time signatures and syncopations, training your ear to recognize and replicate them accurately.

By advancing your ear training proficiency, you'll gain the ability to play music by ear, improvise with greater confidence, and deepen your understanding of musical structures. This skill is invaluable for any guitarist looking to enhance their overall musicianship and creative potential.

Lesson 25: Learning Solos From Recordings

Learning solos from recordings is an invaluable skill for any lead guitarist. It allows you to understand the nuances of different playing styles, improve your technique, and expand your musical vocabulary.

Strategies for Transcribing Solos

Transcribing solos from recordings involves listening carefully and accurately capturing each note and phrase. This skill develops your ear and deepens your understanding of musical structure and expression.

- **Active Listening**: Begin by listening to the solo several times to familiarize yourself with its overall structure, style, and mood.

Focus on different aspects with each listen, such as the melody, rhythm, or phrasing. Take note of any standout sections or techniques that catch your attention.

- **Breaking Down the Solo:** Divide the solo into manageable sections, such as phrases or bars. Work on transcribing each section individually, focusing on accuracy

Use audio software to slow down the recording without altering the pitch, which can help you discern fast or complex passages more easily.

- **Using Tools:** Leverage technology to assist in transcribing. Software and apps can help isolate parts, loop sections, and adjust playback speed.

These tools can be invaluable for capturing intricate solos and ensuring you accurately replicate what you hear.

Techniques for Mastering Solos

Once you have transcribed a solo, mastering it on your instrument requires patience and practice. This topic will cover methods for internalizing and performing the solo with confidence and style.

- **Slow Practice and Gradual Speed Increase:** Start by playing the solo slowly, focusing on clean note production and precise articulation.

Use a metronome to ensure consistent timing. Gradually increase the tempo as you become more comfortable, aiming for both speed and accuracy.

- **Attention to Detail:** Pay close attention to the nuances of the original performance, such as dynamics, vibrato, and bends.

These details contribute to the solo's expressiveness. Emulate these elements to capture the essence of the solo while adding your personal touch.

- **Incorporating Techniques:** Use the solo as an opportunity to practice and refine various guitar techniques.

Identify challenging sections that require specific skills, such as alternate picking or legato, and focus on improving these areas through targeted exercises.

- **Performance and Interpretation:** Once you have mastered the technical aspects, focus on delivering the solo with emotion and confidence. Consider the song's context and the original artist's intent.

Also, allow your interpretation to shine through. Recording yourself can provide valuable feedback on your progress and help refine your performance.

By learning solos from recordings, you'll enhance your technical skills, expand your musical repertoire, and develop a deeper appreciation for different playing styles. This ability is a powerful tool on your journey as a lead guitarist, enriching your music-making and performance.

Chapter VIII Quiz

In Chapter 8, you learned about setting goals, developing practice habits, proficient ear training, and learning solos from recordings. All designed to enhance your musicianship.

Q: How can creating short-term guitar goals be beneficial?

A: ____

Q: How can creating long-term guitar goals be beneficial?

A; ____

Q: What is a key component in an effective practice routine?

A: ____

Q: How do you maintain motivation in your guitar practice?

A: ____

Q: What is the benefit of recognizing note intervals by ear?

A; ____

Q: How can you benefit from learning solos from recordings?

A: ____

Chapter VIII Summary

<u>First,</u> you learn about setting guitar goals. Setting clear and achievable guitar goals is essential for progressing as a lead guitarist. By defining your objectives, you can focus your practice effectively and track your growth over time.

<u>Second</u>, you learn about setting short-term and long-term guitar goals. Understanding the difference between short-term and long-term goals is crucial for creating a structured practice regimen that fosters continuous improvement.

<u>Third</u>, you learn how to develop practice habits. Establishing effective practice habits is crucial for any guitarist striving to progress and achieve their musical goals. An effective practice routine is the backbone of your development as a guitarist.

<u>Fourth</u>, you learn about ear training proficiency. Developing ear-training proficiency is an essential skill for any guitarist, enabling you to recognize musical elements by ear and enhance your improvisation and composition.

<u>Lastly</u>, by continuing your journey as a guitarist, you can grow your skills, deepen your appreciation for music, improve your overall musicianship, and share what you've learned with others.

Lead Guitar Mastery: Conclusion

Congratulations on reaching the end of the "Beginner's Guide to Lead Guitar Mastery"! As you have progressed through this guide, you have been equipped with a diverse array of techniques and insights designed to elevate your playing.

From foundational skills like alternate picking and understanding the musical alphabet, to popular concepts, each lesson serves as a building block to hone your craft and express your unique musical voice.

Throughout your learning journey, the emphasis on both technical proficiency and creative expression underscores the importance of balance in becoming a well-rounded lead guitarist and musician.

Mastery of scales, such as the major and minor pentatonic, and the ability to improvise over classic progressions like the 12-bar blues, are crucial for developing your improvisational skills and expressing your lead guitar prowess.

Equally important is cultivating effective practice habits and a growth mindset. By setting clear goals, maintaining consistent practice routines, and embracing challenges, you can ensure continuous improvement in your playing.

Remember also to share your passion and knowledge with others. Whether through collaborative performances, jam sessions, or teaching, sharing your skills can inspire those around you.

Embrace the joy of discovery and the endless possibilities that music offers. With determination and creativity, your journey toward lead guitar mastery will be fulfilling, transformative, and enriching, not only your life but also those who experience your music.

To all your success,

Sincerely, Dwayne Jenkins

Other Books From Dwayne Jenkins

Learn Guitar Scale Theory:

Dive deep into guitar scale theory with this easy to learn from, comprehensive guidebook. An understanding of theory can add a rich vocabulary for both harmony and melody.

Learning guitar scale theory will help you expand your improvisation skills, enhance your scale vocabulary, and deepen your understanding of intervals.

Demystifying the Blues Scales:

After mastering the pentatonic scales, I recommend you learn the blues scales. These utilize the "blue" note that allows you to expand your versatility in creating solos and melodies.

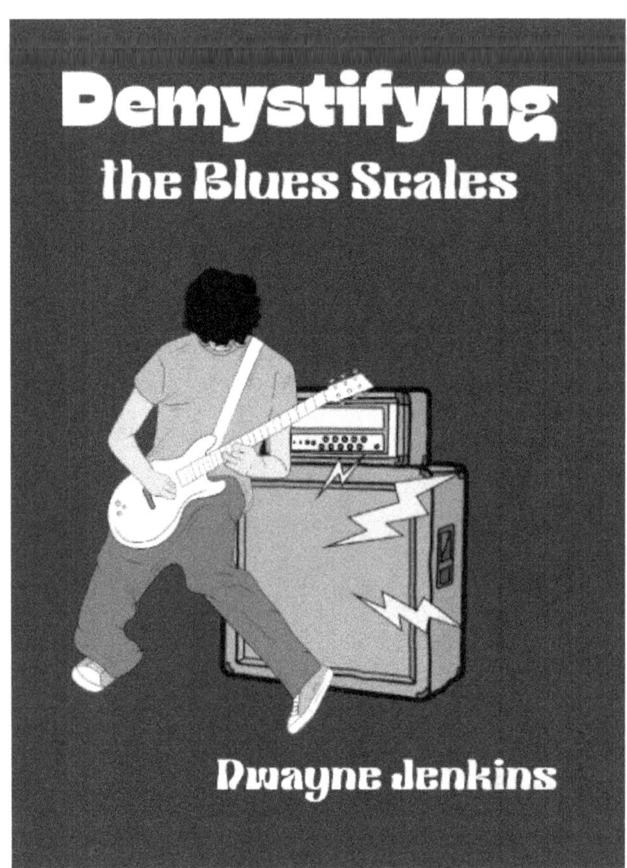

With step-by-step instructions, diagrams, notation, and exercises. All that will be needed is your desire to learn and time to practice. Explore the fun of playing the blues.

Learn Guitar Chord Theory:

If you'd like to learn more about chord theory and enhance your knowledge of chord construction, this book will do it. A great way to expand your guitar chord vocabulary.

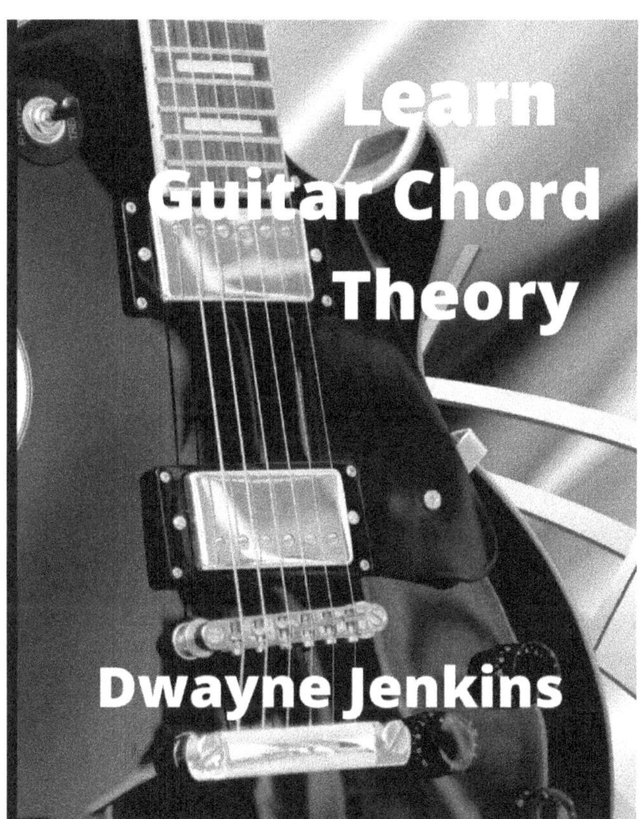

Learn Guitar Chord Theory is a comprehensive study guide on the inner workings of guitar chords, with step-by-step lessons, diagrams, exercises, and learning assessments. All designed to unlock the mysteries of the fretboard.

All books are authored by Dwayne Jenkins, published by Tritone Publishing, and are available worldwide.

Digital formats of all titles are available for instant learning. Just download them to your computer and start learning anywhere, anytime.

Self-study is a great way to learn, as it allows you not only to go at your own pace but also to develop self-discipline and time management, which can benefit you in other areas of your life.

Also, check out Dwayne's Guitar Lessons video channel on YouTube. These are free lessons covering a wide range of guitar topics.

Whether you are working on rhythm, lead, theory, or guitar maintenance, it is all here in these lessons. These are available 24 hours a day, 7 days a week, 365 days a year.

If more help is needed, Dwayne also offers one-on-one coaching on his website.

www.DwaynesGuitarLessons.com

Best of luck, and be sure to have fun.

About the Author

Dwayne Jenkins is a guitar teacher with a unique, engaging approach that helps students of all ages and skill levels enjoy playing the guitar and ukulele. His enthusiasm and love for teaching shine through every lesson that he creates.

His lessons are designed to help you progress. No matter your reason for learning, there will always be something in Dwayne's books and products to help you achieve your dreams.

So if you're a student looking to start or a student looking to further your education, be sure to get involved with Dwayne's guitar lessons and learn what so many people have already discovered: why learning to play the guitar is one of the most incredible things you can do for yourself.

What Students Are Saying About Dwayne's Guitar Lessons

"Dwayne, thank you so much for everything you have taught me and done for me. You are an amazing guitarist and wonderful teacher". BJ.

"Dwayne, it has been a true pleasure to have you at our house each week! Ken & Trevor have learned so much through you and your teachings. Thank you!" Lisa.

"Dwayne, thank you for being a great teacher and teaching me many great songs. This is a skill that will last me a lifetime." Danielle.

"Dwayne, we want you to know we are honored to have you at the studio. We appreciate all that you do and are grateful that we can leave you in charge." Angie & Wilson M.E.C.

"Dwayne, we are so glad you are our Teacher. It's been three years already, can you believe it? Thank you again. You're the best!" Chelsey & Lucas.

"Dwayne, we are so glad that you are in our lives. Chelsey & Lucas enjoy their time with you and look up to you. Looking forward to another great year! Love and best wishes, Ken & Sue.

"Dwayne, thank you so much for being not only an awesome guitar teacher but an awesome friend as well," Kayla.

"Dwayne, thank you so much for all the years of doing lessons. You have been very patient with my progress, helped me build confidence, and inspired me to pursue my dreams. And in doing so, you have become a great friend." Jake.

"Dwayne, thank you for teaching Nick guitar so well. He loves it and is getting quite good, fast. I'm amazed!" Jane.

"Dwayne, thank you so much for teaching me every Saturday, and not only teaching me guitar but also about life, and helping me with setting my goals. You are a great teacher, mentor, and the best friend ever." Carson.

"There is no other person I would want to teach me a guitar! His 1-on-1 teaching makes learning guitar very personal & exhilarating. He teaches at your pace and takes pride in what YOU want to learn. The best part is that if Dwayne doesn't know a song a student wants to play, he takes time out of the week to learn it. His teaching comes to life in my performance and has progressed over the last 8 years. Words cannot describe how amazing a teacher, rockstar, and true friend Dwayne has become to me." Dominic.

Resource Guide

The Major and Minor Scales

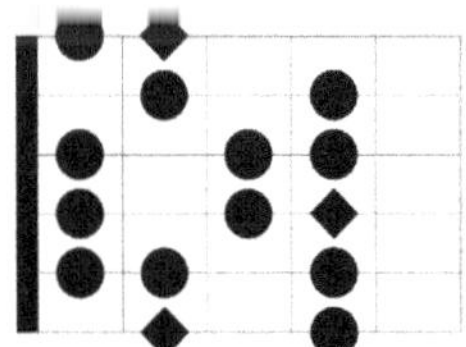

The Major Scale

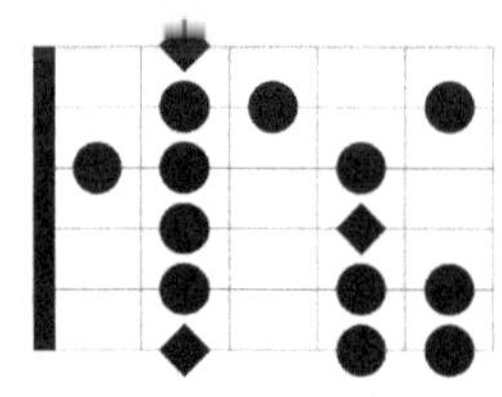

The Natural Minor

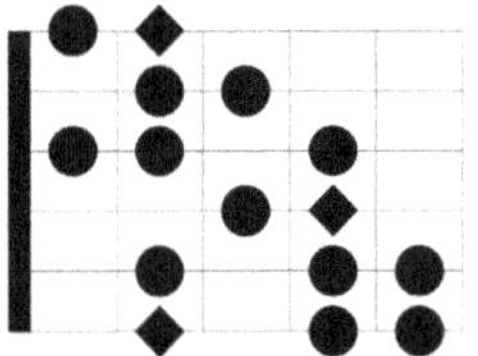

The Harmonic Minor

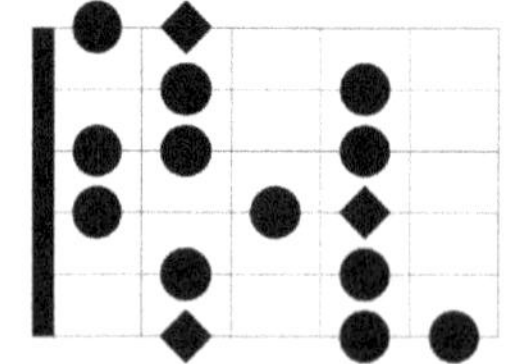

The Melodic Minor

The Major Scale: 1 2 3 4 5 6 7 Octave

The Natural Minor Scale: 1 2 b3 4 5 b6 b7 Octave

The Harmonic Minor Scale: 1 2 b3 4 5 b6 7 Octave

The Melodic Minor Scale: 1 2 b3 4 5 6 7 Octave

Each minor scale produces a different shade of color.

Resource Guide Continued

The Five Major Pentatonic Scales

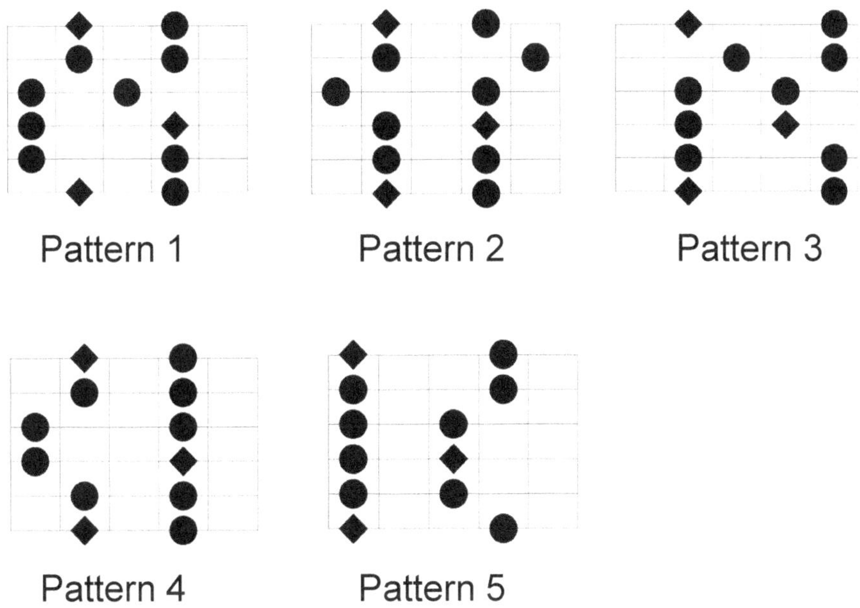

Pattern 1   Pattern 2   Pattern 3

Pattern 4   Pattern 5

Things to remember:

1. It is a five-note scale that produces a bright, happy sound.
2. The number value is 1 2 3 5 6.
3. Key Example, C Major: C D E G A
4. Created by eliminating the 4th and 7th notes of the major.
5. Each pattern starts on a tone degree of the scale.

Master all five scale patterns in both major and minor.

142

The Five Minor Pentatonic Scales

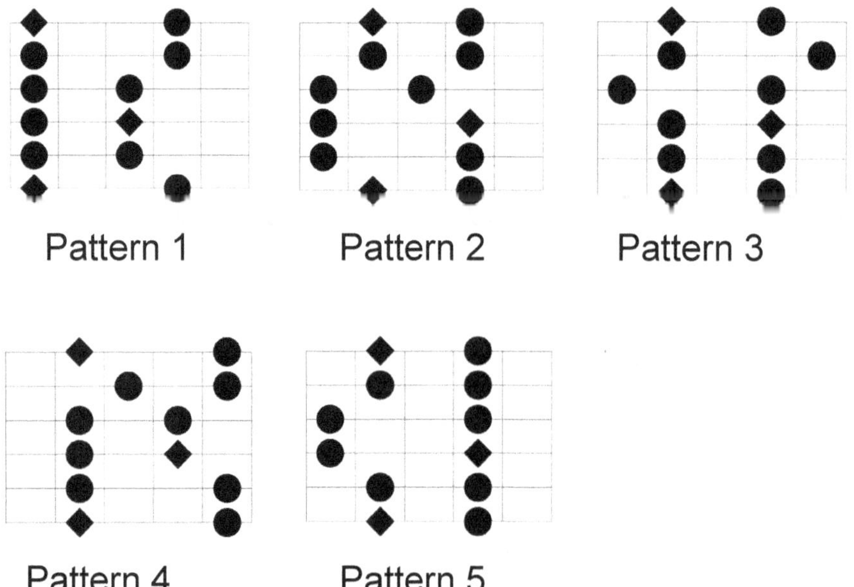

1. It is a five-note scale that produces a sad, somber sound.
2. The number value is 1 b3 4 5 b7
3. Key example, A minor: A C D E G
4. Created by eliminating the 2nd and 6th of the major.
5. Each pattern starts on a tone degree of the scale.

These five-note scale patterns are essential for lead guitar mastery. Once you get these down, move on to mastering the blues scales and the modes.

Although simple, do not overlook their potency. Many great blues and rock guitarists use them.

Resource Guide Continued

Common Chords

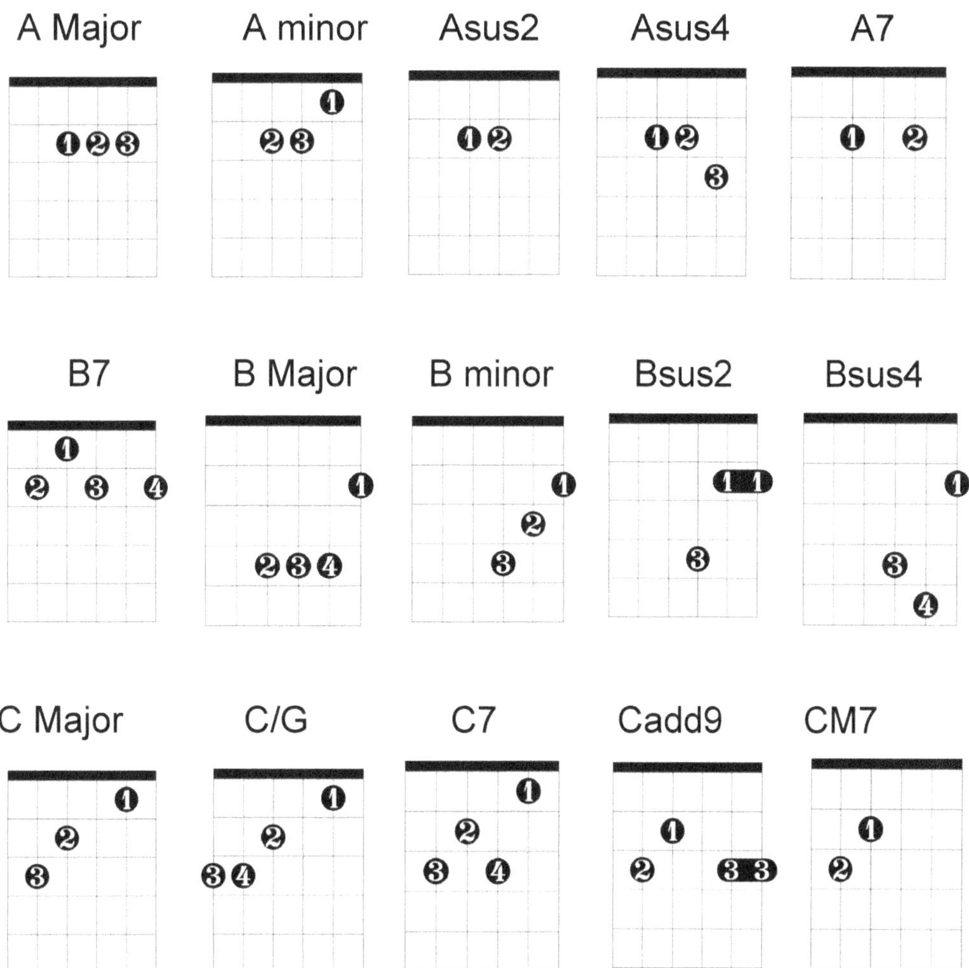

These are all chords found in many of your favorite songs.
Learn them and have them handy for when needed.

Resource Guide Continued

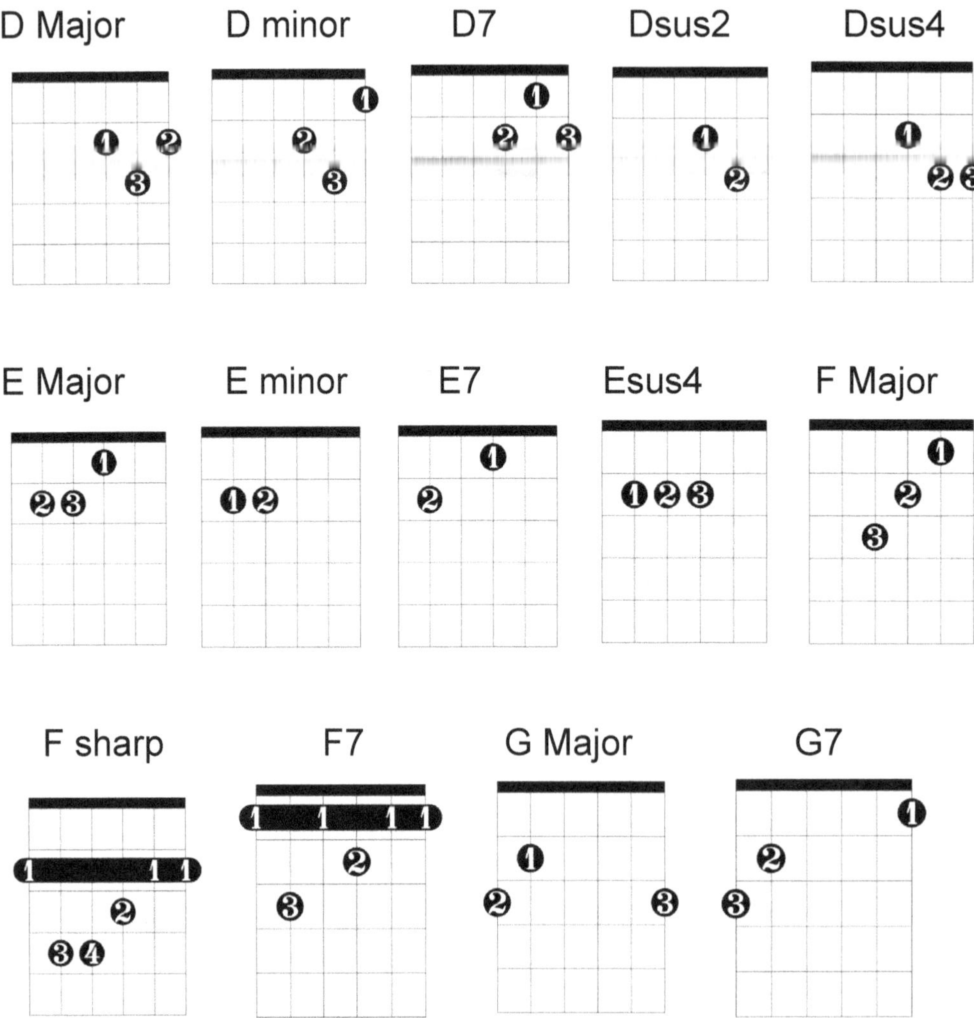

Remember, the F sharp and F7 are barre chords and are played with your index finger barring across all six strings. Not easy to start with, but very beneficial in the long run.

Resource Guide Continued

The I-IV-V Chords in Multiple Keys

Key	I	IV	V
C	C	F	G
D	D	G	A
E	E	A	B
F	F	Bb	C
G	G	C	D
A	A	D	E
B	B	E	F#

This diagram shows you what chords will be best to use in these particular keys. These are the most common keys and chords that will be found in songs.

This makes an excellent quick reference guide. Remember, you can use the other chords within the key as well, but these are the ones I recommend you start with.

Experiment with these chords over the 12-bar blues progression. As you do so, your ear will become familiar with them, and you will hear how songs are constructed with them, which will give you ideas for constructing your own musical compositions.

Resource Guide Continued

Notes Within Common Major Keys: W-W-H-W-W-W-H

1. A Major: A B C# D E F# G# octave
2. B major: B C# D# E F# G# A# octave
3. C Major: C D E F G A B octave
4. D Major: D E F# G A B C# octave
5. E Major: E F# G# A B C# D# octave
6. F Major: F G A Bb C D E octave
7. G Major: G A B C D E F# octave

Notes Within Common Minor Keys: W-H-W-W-H-W-W

1. A minor: A B C D E F G octave
2. B minor: B C# D E F# G A octave
3. C minor: C D Eb F G Ab Bb octave
4. D minor: A Bb C D E F G octave
5. E minor: E F# G A B C D octave
6. F minor: F G Ab Bb C Db Eb octave
7. G minor: G A Bb C D Eb F octave

Two Extra Common Minor Keys: W-H-W-W-H-W-W

1. B flat minor: Bb C Db Eb F Gb Ab
2. F sharp minor: F# G# A B C# D E

All the information in this resource guide has been covered in the training and presented here for easier reference. All scales presented are commonly found in many songs in many styles of music.

Chords covered in the training are presented, as well as others that are commonly found in many songs. Once you learn to read chord charts, I recommend you learn all the chords and add them to your vocabulary.

Notes within common keys are also presented to help you understand the inner workings of musical keys. You will encounter these in your playing, and they will help you better understand scale and chord construction.

The more chords and scales you have in your guitar playing arsenal, the better you'll be at figuring out songs and composing ones of your own. Making you a well-rounded musician.